Praise for
Ascend Your Start-Up

"In this helpful guide, Helen parlays decades of experience scaling and advising start-ups into practical, actionable advice for any B2B start-up team."

—Clara Shih
Founder of Hearsay Systems;
CEO of Salesforce Service Cloud

"Start-up veterans know that a start-up cannot succeed without a mindset relentlessly attuned to experiments and pivots. *Ascend Your Start-Up* arms readers with a requisite framework to prepare them for the challenging journey through every stage of growth."

—Eva Tsai
Marketing Executive at Google Cloud;
Start-Up Board Director and Advisor

"I recommend Helen Yu's book *Ascend Your Start-Up* for its great insights to scale your business."

—Spiros Margaris
VC / Ranked Global No. 1 Finance Influencer
by Refinitiv (Thomson Reuters) & Ranked Global No. 1
Fintech, AI, Blockchain & No. 2 InsurTech
Influencer by Onalytica

"As a start-up founder, you often encounter all varieties of challenges and growth disconnects that prevent your business from scaling. *Ascend Your Start-Up* strategically helps you bridge those disconnects and thoughtfully forces you to reflect on your business in a productive manner."

—Jonathan Lacoste
Co-Founder of Jebbit; Forbes 30 Under 30

"*Ascend Your Start-Up* is the holy grail for start-up founders, growth-minded executives, and turnaround leaders. Helen's provides both pragmatic guidance and a playbook that's required reading for every industry."

—R "Ray" Wang
CEO, Constellation Research,
Inc. & Best-Selling Author

"I was fired up to see Helen building a practical guide based upon her decades of experience around managing the various phases of growth in a company's trajectory. Read it so you can avoid the pitfalls!"

—Nick Mehta
CEO, Gainsight

"Helen Yu's practical guide for growing and scaling businesses is a must-read for all entrepreneurs."

—Shellye Archambeau
Former CEO, MetricStream; BOD, Verizon;
Fortune Top 10 Business Book Author

"*Ascend Your Start-Up* provides a clear framework for anticipating and overcoming the central disconnects that unlock growth in start-ups and Fortune 500 innovation centers alike. Helen's vast experience and ability to convey complex issues in a concise manner makes this a must-read."

—Jason Holmes
Managing Director, Nomad Advisors LLC;
Former Interim CEO, COO, Marketo

"I have been involved with venture back start-ups on a global level for over 20 years. I have learned a lot, and this knowledge helped me be part of two IPOs and a successful trade sale to Oracle. Navigating a start-up to a scale-up requires resilience, patience, and execution. Helen is an insightful and experienced executive who has witnessed firsthand the journey that early stage companies take. Her book is a pragmatic asset to any executive embarking along the journey of building a successful company. This book is like having an experienced advisor / sounding board in the palm of your hand. A highly recommended read."

—Lawrence Whittle
CEO, Parsable Inc.

"A must-read for founders to learn from and avoid the errors and pitfalls that lead most start-ups to fail. A practical guide for an entrepreneur's journey."

—Dev Ganesan
CEO, PathFactory

"Get unstuck and reclaim your start-up's mojo with the brilliance of *Ascend Your Start-Up*! Helen Yu spills the beans on tested success formulas for scaling up your start-up in her latest book!"

—Ajay Awatramani
Chief Product Officer, Cornerstone On Demand;
Former Head of B2B Strategy and Product, Adobe

"All founders, especially first-time founders, need to master the art of asking the right questions. Helen's greatest strength is her ability to ask the right questions and help founders uncover the answers they need. Helen worked with my co-founder and I during a critical 2-year period and helped us successfully pivot our business by challenging us in all the right ways with the questions we needed to hear."

—Tom Coburn
CEO and Co-Founder of Jebbit; Forbes 30 Under 30

"The ethical, just, and effective intersection of humanity and tech is one of the most important endeavors of our time. Helen embodies that intersection. As a tech CEO and founder myself, her book is the perfect guide as we build modern companies for scale in a world where purpose is everything."

—Coco Brown
Founder and CEO, Athena Alliance, Inc.

"Helen Yu will help firms beat the odds with a successful launch. Inspiring to the greatest heights with her authentic and personal story of loyalty, dedication, and strength of character, *Ascend Your Start-Up* is a must-read for start-ups and Fortune 500 executives alike."

—Martin Tang
Chairman, Global Cybersecurity Association, Switzerland

"*Ascend Your Start-Up* arms readers with checklists and practical questions to ask throughout the start-up journey. Written with an adventurous backdrop, it captures the challenges and rewards of moving methodically through every stage of growth."

—Cynthia Plouche
Board of Directors; ESG Enthusiast

ASCEND YOUR START-UP

Conquer the **5** Disconnects to

ACCELERATE GROWTH

HELEN YU

MADE FOR SUCCESS

Made for Success Publishing
P.O. Box 1775 Issaquah, WA 98027
www.MadeForSuccessPublishing.com

Distributed by Made for Success Publishing

First Printing

Library of Congress Cataloging-in-Publication data
Yu, Helen
    ASCEND YOUR START-UP: Conquer the 5 Disconnects to Accelerate Growth
    p. cm.

LCCN: 2021934940

ISBN: 978-1-64146-621-9 (*Hardback*)
ISBN: 978-1-64146-648-6 (*Audiobook*)
ISBN: 978-1-64146-631-8 (*eBook*)

Printed in the United States of America

For further information contact Made for Success Publishing
+14255266480 or email service@madeforsuccess.net

Contents

FOREWORD

I have been in the Hospitality industry for over 40 years and have experience in Retail as well. I have been leading operational growth in various parts of the world and have built financial infrastructures for large private and public companies. For a number of years, I have also been in charge of technology for one of the big brands in Hospitality. Through that work, I have had the pleasure of getting to know Helen Yu, and we have been in touch for over 20 years.

Helen is an extraordinary person; she has strong interpersonal skills and a deep understanding of how people function and can drive organizations to explore their full potential. She is focused and precise in her analysis and assessments and has proven numerous times the impact she leaves on organizations is exponential. In her book, *Ascend Your Start-Up*, she explains how one can accelerate growth by applying focus and simple principles to unlock the potential of an organization. The book is fascinating in its clear, precise, and easy-to-digest way of describing the disconnects to accelerate growth, allowing an immediate correlation to many situations start-up founders and CEOs live through every day. It is absolutely a must-read for someone starting up a business and looking for avenues of fast acceleration—or those who find themselves at a point of stagnation and in need of new inspiration for growth.

With her tremendous experience and success in business, an innate understanding of what drives people and where the potential pitfalls and shortcomings are, Helen is the perfect Sherpa for her readers.

Every conversation I've ever had with Helen has been fascinating, causing me to explore new ways of thinking, new angles to look at situations, and different assessments of challenges to explore opportunities for growth and success. Helen is incredibly articulate in her speaking engagements, and she has used those communication skills to lay it all out in this book. Believe me when I say that *Ascend Your Start-Up* is a must-read for anybody looking for inspiration in business growth!

Gebhard F. Rainer
CEO, Sandals Resorts International Inc.

INTRODUCTION

The first thing I noticed about Jebbit co-founders Jonathan Lacoste and Tom Coburn was their maturity and dedication to their business despite looking so young. Both are extremely bright with high emotional intelligence. Jonathan could have been a young Brad Pitt or an earnest-looking Neil Armstrong, tall in stature with an easy-going smile. Tom might have been coming over on a Friday night to play video games. In fact, on Jebbit's site, Tom's bio picture features him holding up his favorite game, Settlers of Catan, which he states he "will play for hours."

They were young, but they were fierce.

Underneath their youthful exuberance was a mature sensibility. I wondered where this aura of being "older" came from and learned that Jonathan had been a nationally ranked ice hockey goaltender—*and* the youngest goaltender to win a game in the North American Hockey League (NAHL) at the age of sixteen.

Both gentlemen took a risky plunge, even for founders. The one-time classmates dropped out of Boston College to start

Jebbit in 2012. Both would become founders of the first-ever declared data SaaS platform. CNBC recognized Jebbit as one of the top 25 most promising companies in the world.[1] Forbes put both co-founders on its 30 Under 30 list, and the company would later attract more than $20 million in investor funding.

Still, there was something wise in these young founders. In one media interview, Jonathan was asked what advice he would give his 20-year-old self. Jonathan responded: "Be more patient. Be more thankful." He didn't have to go back that far—his "twenty-year-old self" had been around for just five years at that point.

The Journey Ahead

Here's the story. In 2016, Tom had reached out to Steve Lucas, the newly appointed CEO of Marketo after it had been acquired by Vista Equity. Tom shared with him that Jebbit had a common customer with Marketo and would like to discuss potential collaboration opportunities. I gave these founders big props for having the guts to reach out and explore collaboration with a $300 million global company. Jebbit had about 20 employees at the time. Steve's answer was to the point: "Anything customer-related is Helen."

Fortuitously, I had to travel to Boston the following week. We met at their college dorm-like offices over coffee.

---

[1]Jebbit Marketing Team, "Jebbit Reflects on Q1 with 4th Consecutive Quarter of Record Revenue Growth," Jebbit.com, Published April 15, 2015, https://www .jebbit.com/blog/jebbit-reflects-q1-4th-consecutive-quarter-record-revenue -growth

"We have a joint customer. How can we further collaborate?" Tom said. His "ask" was the first step to open up a tremendous opportunity for Jebbit. That's one of many reasons I admire both Jonathan and Tom. They are brilliant, yes, but many founders are brilliant technologists and visionaries on a grand scale. These traits alone are not enough. No, Jonathan and Tom had something more.

They had an insatiable hunger to learn. They were never arrogant. In every conversation, they always told me what they *didn't* know. Not a single moment did they come off as knowing all the answers. To learn, one must be an active listener and turn information into actionable insight. They did this in spades. Most founders are curious learners, but not all listen, bringing back fresh ideas to their team and then taking action.

There is no perfect DNA for a founder. Each person comes out of the gate with a unique set of experiences and beliefs, talents and expertise, likes and dislikes. As founder of my own consulting firm, Tigon Advisory, I am no exception.

I've studied this question for many years. The answer became the basis for my own business and the realization that the missing pieces—the disconnects—are what holds us back in life.

I talked straight with Tom. "Before we jump into that customer and how to collaborate, could you share the Jebbit story with me, and what your top challenges are?"

Through that first one-hour conversation, I learned an incredible amount about Jebbit—and about Tom. I asked a ton of questions and was quite touched by Tom's self-aware-ness of what skills he did *not* have. He listened really well, and was thoughtful when responding to my questions. I realized how much growth potential Jebbit has and how much I could help by leveraging my decades of experience.

It was difficult. My role was not to hand over answers because the answers were *inside* them. My goal was to tease them out through exploration. So, I did this by challenging them with questions like:

What is your longer-term vision?

Who is your ideal customer profile?

Does your solution solve the problem your ideal customers have?

Will you stay with these verticals, or will you expand?

Are you willing to pivot if you need to, or are you married to the original idea?

I spent the next two years as an advisor to Jebbit. We spent most of that time unpacking their go-to-market strategy, which meant one thing: asking a lot of questions.

The Milestones

Exploring questions is much more important to a founder than having ready-made answers handed to them (which is precisely why *Ascend Your Start-Up* is a decision framework made up of, you guessed it, questions). Assumptions are the greatest enemy for a start-up founder.

With that said, this is not a book that will teach you how to write a business plan, a product launch plan, an investor pitch deck, or any strategic document. The questions outlined in this decision framework cannot be Googled or found in one place for the simple reason that many of these questions pull back the curtain and reflect the unspoken challenges faced by founders. You will dive into what keeps founders up at one in the morning rather than how best to pitch an investor or write a great job description. You will see the most common disconnects, sometimes as simple as thinking of things out of order, like waiting to focus on brand rather than instilling it into your product, that add to the statistic that 90 percent of start-ups fail.[1]

Tom and Jonathan have a lot of shared values; they are hard-working, open to new ideas, and humble. They assembled a good team of advisors as they grew, and this continues today. They took on the challenging questions and sought to find answers. Jonathan would get up early and be in the library by seven in the morning oftentimes. Tom sometimes called at ten at night with questions when he was just wrapping up work. They were young, yes, but they were truly fierce in their hunger for knowledge.

There was a micro-moment, though, that was particularly telling. The founders were in a tough spot. When they started in 2011, there were 100 marketing technology companies. Five years later, when we met at their offices in Boston, there were 7,000 MarTech (Marketing Technology) companies. How do you set yourself apart from the competition?

[1]Kyril Kotashev, "Startup Failure Rate: Ultimate Report+Infographic [2020]," Failory.com, Published March 17, 2018, https://www.failory.com/blog/startup-failure-rate

One late summer evening, they called me and asked a crucial question: "At what point do you need a customer success team, and how do you structure your organization to scale?" They had an RFP with a major e-retailer. Up to that point, they had historically served smaller customers and didn't have a pricing structure for a large, publicly held company. They had to pivot. Soon after, I found myself sitting with Jonathan in an office lobby in San Francisco. We went through the customer journey in different phases of growth. We talked about the importance of aligning with big players: Salesforce, Adobe, and Marketo. They had the capability to partner with large MarTech companies to increase conversion rates, and they did. Integrations with big players fueled their growth.

They realized, after much soul-searching, they had to swim in a different lane to reach the same destination. What would you have done in their position? How easily could you have abandoned everything you knew to dramatically reduce your number of clients while completely renovating your pricing model? In a way, this massive pivot was like leaving one's homeland and building a new life in another country. But hard things can oftentimes be the right things.

The Roadmap

Jonathan and Tom's story shows what successful leaders look like. Both admitted to me that they knew the hard road ahead, but were devoted to pivoting from MarTech to data declaration because they could stand out and gain market share in ways they never could before. That's how they differentiated themselves from a thousand other companies.

Micro-moments are the key steps to achieving a milestone. You must seize those moments. In this book, you will learn about many, many micro-moments of growth. You might not be able to see how critical they are when you look at them individually, but they set the tone on how you drive growth forward. Tom and Jonathan's spirit and gut brought them to the mountain. But that is not enough for you to make the climb. You must pick the right Sherpa and guide to help you on your journey (after all, you don't know what you don't know and it could be dangerous), be over-prepared to the point of exhaustion, and be willing to go backward at the right moment in order to move your company forward.

You might think that after working with Tom and Jonathan and other founders that I got super-motivated to write a book that would save them all from sleepless nights and needless pain. Not true. At the onset of writing *Ascend Your Start-Up*, I realized that it was completely impossible to write one book for flawlessly scaling the start-up mountain. No one book will ever cover every footstep of a founder's ascent. The reason is not for lack of knowledge on the part of any one author, but rather that each climb is different.

What Does it Take to Grow?

"What has marked your personal journey? What traits have helped bring you to this moment?" I get asked these questions often. There are three traits that have defined my journey:

1. Curiosity
2. Grit
3. Being a risk-taker

I started my career as an accountant and financial analyst. From there, every job I held meant learning an entirely new set of skills, a new industry, or a new side to business. Curiosity and learning opened up new worlds for me. I learned to code as a Hyperion consultant and went on to design and implement 400+ financial planning and reporting applications working alongside CFOs.

Being a risk-taker has led me to share my love of learning and knowledge with others. In every position, I've accepted the challenge that comes with uncharted waters. I ran an Oracle BI consulting practice post-acquisition with the added pleasure of learning from then-Oracle Executive Vice President of Sales Keith Block. Under his tutelage, I learned the nuances of Enterprise Solution Sales at Oracle. At Adobe, I then learned marketing and SaaS and successfully led the start-up to scale-up challenges at Marketo.

In fact, my journey led me to recognize critical gap patterns in growth-driven technology companies, prompting me to become an entrepreneur of a growth accelerator called Tigon Advisory.

Are You Ready for the Journey to Scale?

My story is not your story. Each start-up founder is different. You are the only you around. Your innovation process is yours alone. Your style is unique. Your need for sleep, your best creative time of day, the primal nature of being an introvert or extrovert, your risk tolerance, your favorite childhood game, your love of writing or your abhorrence of it, your single-hood or vast parental responsibilities, your education or lack thereof—all these things make you who you are. No one book can be one-size-fits-all. The prize is different for each founder. Not all climbers aim for the summit. In fact, the "summit" or goal may change as time goes on.

One thing common to all founders, though, is the path of complex decisions that must be made in order to scale. While all these decisions may not apply to you, most of them will. This book gives you a decision framework to scale faster and more fearlessly, faster and more gracefully, faster and more sanely.

Let's unpack this a bit. In the more than 500 conversations I've had with founders, I haven't found a single person who doesn't want to grow faster. No one has ever said to me, "Hey, Helen, I hope my start-up takes 10 years to scale," or "My runway extends all the way to the millennium. We've got loads of time. Let's grab lunch and talk about the Cubs." (I had to get to my hometown Chicago somehow!)

No, these are not typical founder soundbites. Instead, there's an urgency to survive and a vision to thrive faced by the start-up founder, and *Ascend Your Start-Up* explores the many crossroads encountered along the way. At each crossroad is a decision you must make that helps or hinders growth. With every answer, you build a stronger, more focused approach to your ascent—and bridge the disconnects that hold you back.

Of course, building a business is no different than life itself—thus the common phrase of describing a business as "your baby." Building a start-up is not without intense emotion. If scaling faster is one part of the equation, the other part is fear.

Unless you are like rock climber Alex Honnold, whose amygdala refuses to trigger sweaty palms and heart palpitations even when he is scaling the flat face of Yosemite National Park's Half Dome or the nose of El Capitan—without a rope—growing a start-up is scary.[1] Unlike Mr. Honnold, made famous by the documentary *Free Solo*, your amygdala (and mine) light up like fireworks in July when things go awry. For the founder, this is an exhaustive list of possibilities. You don't have a playbook. You don't have a lot of time. You risk running out of money and exhausting your resources before your product sticks.

If you choose the wrong path to your customer amidst the hairy web of marketing choices, you have a ringside seat to watching money, some of which belongs to other people, actually evaporate before your eyes. You must place your bets on key people, and sometimes those bets pay nothing. If all that isn't scary enough, you put your integrity on the line and sacrifice family time, and even time to take care of *yourself*. Unless you are endowed with a handsome trust fund, start-up founders oftentimes make bet-the-house moves to scale.

---

[1] J.B. MacKinnon, "The Strange Brain of the World's Greatest Solo Climber," Pocket, Published June 28, 2018, https://getpocket.com/explore/item/the-strange -brain-of-the-world-s-greatest-solo-climber

With growth comes risk, and with risk comes fear, a human emotion that is perfectly normal. Mountaineer Alison Levine explores this word further: "Fear only becomes dangerous when it paralyzes you." Fear's alter ego is confidence, and one of the best ways to inspire her is to be prepared. I call this scaling your start-up "gracefully." To be fearless is to climb a mountain without a rope. To be graceful is to climb the mountain *with* the rope—and all the other tools, advisors, vision, and practices you need—and conquer it, perhaps not fearlessly, but always with great courage.

To prepare you for your journey was the real reason I wrote this book.

My Personal Journey

Your company is not a hobby or craft project operating from your garage. This is real, and that perhaps is the scariest part of all. So, while this book will help you scale faster, it will also help you scale more fearlessly; more sanely. When you reach your Summit, my hope is that you've made it with a little less pain and a little more confidence than you otherwise would have had.

Ninety percent of start-ups fail because they don't see their growth disconnects—those broken or weakened links barring a company from moving forward. This might be turning a blind eye to an unhealthy work culture or an over-emphasis on policy over customer experience, or targeting too large of an audience. This book explores those disconnects—and not only that, but the dozens of micro-decisions that must be made along the way in order to scale without sacrificing yourself, the people you love, and the company you are passionate about.

In these pages, I've overlaid my 14-day expedition to reach Mount Everest's base camp on the North Col in Tibet, which is 17,000 feet above sea level, as a metaphor for the start-up journey. The last three days were the hardest. When you are at such high altitudes, there is 50 percent less oxygen.[1] The trek was both slippery and surprising (with an occasional yak rearing its head unexpectedly), not to mention intimidating. In the end, Mount Everest was a beast to climb. So is founding a tech start-up.

Everest has challenged many climbers, of which more than 5,000 have successfully summited. Mountain climbing is, in effect, a series of interrelated decisions and activities that get you to the summit—and, equally important—help you descend safely. For the founder, all roads lead to growth by confidence in preparing our business ecosystems through a framework of decisions. As you dig into the pages of the book you have in your hands, regard this as an expedition—no different than climbing Mount Everest, which is why I've chosen to use my own mountaineering adventure as a backdrop. Scaling a mountain and scaling a company call for similar attributes. Here, we will talk about building the tech start-up using what I learned climbing that very tall mountain that has bewitched and challenged climbers over the years, bringing many to their death.

---

[1] "How hard is it to trek Everest Base Camp?" Adventurealternative.com https://www.adventurealternative.com/adventure-blog/how-hard-is-it-to-trek-to-everest-base-camp\

As you read on, you'll find each section focuses on questions to explore relative to that leg of the journey. Each chapter includes the emotions many founders feel at each stage of the climb, the decisions critical to advancing forward, and an end-of-chapter summary called "Your Checklist," which gives you an at-a-glance look at each chapter's most important points.

Chapter One: Starting in the Valley of Disconnects will help you get clear on why you are making the journey—and the five biggest disconnects that could potentially hinder your progress.

Chapter Two: Turn Idea into Product Camp helps you explore the critical role of defining your MVP (minimal viable product). This part of your ascent is when you crystallize what problem your product solves, for whom, and why. You will also focus on what kind of company you want to build by mapping out your culture, value, and brand.

Chapter Three: Move Product to Market Camp helps you define your minimal viable team, a pivot moment that moves you upward and onward along the slippery slope up the scale-up mountain.

Chapter Four: Go from Market to Scale Camp helps you build an engine to drive repeatable sales by intentionally driving responsible growth and not leaving it to chance. Repeatability is what takes you from market to scale.

Chapter Five: Acclimate to the Voice of Your Customer Camp gives you the tools and insight you need to explore why your customer invests in you and reveals their decision-making process. Discover how to leverage customer insights to unlock growth potential for you and your customers, as well as figure out your MVR (minimal viable repeatability).

Chapter Six: Align Strategy with Process and Measurement Camp will help you uncover the Process Disconnect and share a framework on how to translate vision into a clear strategy about what actions to take and what actions to avoid. We will look at one of the fiercest challenges to overcome, the Measurement Disconnect, where holding your team accountable and establishing metrics is your top imperative.

Chapter Seven: The Summit: A View Toward Your Next Peak exposes truthful insight about reaching the top and prepares you mentally for the path ahead.

While writing this book, I received a note from someone who said that I had "inspired him as a person" and that he will never forget the "trust and confidence" I put in him. My heart shifted. I was so grateful. To me, my "why" has always been and will continue to be multiplying the success, joy, and dreams of others. Doing so is never a one-way street. It is always two lanes, a dialogue of giving and receiving. We have that choice, and it's a wonderful choice. So, most of all, as we embark upon this climb together, I am grateful to you, the courageous and starry-eyed, wise and resilient tech start-up founder. You are *my* Sherpa. My wish for you is to make the best decisions along the way, so you reach your Summit faster and more fearlessly.

The start-up mountain is large, even treacherous. But you can climb this peak if you consider one decision at a time, always in that state of "constant evolution." Armed with the knowledge you are about to learn, you will reach the Summit—*your* Summit—as only you define your white-capped mountain peak.

Time to scale this beast.

Chapter 1

STARTING IN THE VALLEY OF DISCONNECTS

I am dizzy. My eyes blur. Then, I sit down.

My frozen hands gently push white iridescent snow around my grandmother's ashes. Amazing how one thought reaches back to pull forth another. I recall my tiny hand tucked inside hers as I was growing up. I was the only girl, the youngest of 10 cousins raised by a woman with no formal education but who mothered a diplomat who eventually went on to marry one, too.

As my parents traveled around the world, representing their home country of China, my grandmother was, in a word, everything to me. The light of the moon guiding my youth, the strength of the stars, the air by which I breathed. I see her now as I reach my goal of climbing Mount Everest. We are at North Base Camp, 17,000 feet above sea level in Tibet, China. We are more than halfway up the beast, the notorious mountain known for stealing lives and creating stories. Like mine. I finish burying her ashes. My sweat adheres to my jeans, and a teal wool sweater sticks to my body like frozen glue. It is hard for me to breathe, and I am dizzy because of the altitude. My brain moves slowly, like I am running against resistance in a pool of clear water. Then, I remember.

I remember my mission, what she asked me to do. I found myself scaling Mount Everest not because I ever wanted to, but because I was *asked* to. My grandmother's final requests to me before she passed away were this: "Stay special, make the world proud, and spread my ashes on a tall mountain." I promised her I would. This is my final act of doing something for her.

Don't screw it up, Helen. You can do this. Don't turn back. Remember why. These are the thoughts I carry up the mountain along with my pickax and pinions.

I use all my energy to put one foot in front of the other. Only experienced, professional climbers ascend farther up the mountain beyond base camp. First-time amateurs, like me, have reached their peak. I am not sure I have the energy to go on. I feel exhausted. Grief takes hold of a person in different ways.

Wherever she is now, I know her expectations are for me to safely see my family again. She fully expects me to perform my best, to survive under all conditions, and to thrive because, as she taught me, every day, we have the privilege of doing big things and scaling tall mountains.

Base Camp: Sharing Ideas and Exploring Disconnects

Preparing for my trip, I was excited to *do* something for her, as if she were still walking this earth of ours. Many people told me I was making a mistake. They told me it was too risky, too dangerous, too unreasonable. *You're crazy. It is a year before the Beijing Olympics. The roads are not fixed yet.*

Like many founders, it is hard for others to understand why a person would voluntarily suffer and put themselves in an extreme environment. Unlike most people, I could not afford any training prior to climbing Mount Everest. Again, like many founders, I bootstrapped my way to Everest. My training: walking, running, exercising, and staying fit every day. These were free and completely in my control. The Palm (smartphone) was released in May of 2007. I could not afford this, either. In fact, I saved every penny I could just to do the trip.

Like founders, I fed my curiosity through books and asking questions of people I knew. I would go to the library, spending hours reading about mountain climbing. I spoke to friends, and they referred people to me. That's how I secured my Sherpa and driver. My parents suggested that we hire a helicopter and drop grandma's ashes on Mt. Everest. I knew taking the easy way out was not what my grandmother was asking me to do. I would not be keeping my sacred promise to her. "Do what you say you will do" is what Grandma taught me. My inner voice was so strong, I didn't hesitate. Grandma was the world to me, so when I lost her, I lost my world. The journey to Everest was a journey to stay special and make Grandma proud.

As a start-up founder, you might recognize the challenges outlined above. People around you may not understand your dream. You might have to forego a paycheck and bootstrap the first few years. But know this: The voice inside you propelling you forward is your guide. It will not fail you—as long as you sidestep the treacherous missteps caused by disconnects.

All start-ups face strategy-to-execution disconnects. These disconnects stand in the way of "where you are" from "where you want to be"—and, just as importantly, where you need to be in order to scale faster and more fearlessly. What if, though, you could identify these disconnects early on? What if you could take action to bridge those gaps within your start-up that otherwise would have held you back from scaling?

There are three legs to the journey of scaling your start-up: Base Camp, Slope, and Summit. Imagine Base Camp as the fun and ultra-exciting stage where you turn an idea into a product. This is where your pulse beats a little faster on the daily. You are constantly creating, sourcing, exploring, dreaming, and pitching. Here, your chief nemesis is the **Product/Market Fit Disconnect,** where a product must prove itself to be marketable in order to be minimally viable.

You cannot, however, stay in Base Camp forever (you would miss all the fun brought on by the hairpin curves and extreme temperatures further up the mountain!). Instead, you must move forward, digging in your heels for the treacherous, slippery slope of taking your product to market when ideas fly and you work a gazillion hours and begin to feel the physical effects of what it means to be a founder. This is the difficult territory where 90 percent of start-ups fail. At this point, you will be called upon to let go of your product and share it with the people who value it the most. Here, you will face the **Minimum Viable Repeatability Disconnect**, both vital for start-ups to set the stage for repeatable success.

The third and final stage is the insanely challenging shift from market to scale. You finally see the Summit—the one you set out to reach or perhaps a new one that has appeared since you started. Along the way, though, you must triumph over the **Customer Voice Disconnect, Process Disconnect, and Measurement Disconnect**. Make it through these, and your efforts to scale are off and running.

The value of understanding start-up disconnects is the secret sauce of start-up founders. You are more prepared to handle the many curve balls thrown your way. You are more confident. You build from the ground up—and not just your product—but your values, mission, vision, and team. Not unlike scaling a mountain, there are stages to scaling. Ascending means moving through six critical "camps" along the start-up mountain. The transition between these camps is what I call a "crossroad." Crossroads connect each evolution of the founder journey. If you've fully explored your disconnects, you will have added strength and much more resilience to scale faster and more fearlessly as you navigate critical crossroads.

Let's take a look at what this means. A crossroad, according to the *Merriam-Webster* dictionary, is defined as:

"The place of intersection of two or more roads."

This, of course, is the literal interpretation of the word. Another definition, an even more important one, is also listed, aptly describing the many crossroads in a founder's journey:

> "A crucial point especially where a decision
> must be made."

A single decision can sometimes have a ripple effect on the rest of the journey—or even determine if the journey continues at all.

If you know where you are weak and are clear on the road-map ahead, though, your disconnects will impact your decision-making at these crossroads and enable you to scale more fluidly and with greater confidence.

Welcome to Base Camp

So, how do you feel? Are you ready to take on gasping lungs and hairpin turns as we climb higher? Sounds exciting, right?

Mountain climbing is, in effect, a series of interrelated decisions and activities that lead you to the summit under high-risk conditions. Knowing your disconnects and being prepared to handle the crossroads that take you higher and higher up the mountain will help you ascend faster and more gracefully. The experience of reaching Mount Everest's base camp is like birthing your first baby. You never forget how you feel about it at that moment. It is exhilarating while exhausting—a classic start-up thrill.

In the beginning stages of starting a business, you don't have money—or at least the proper funding it needs. Instead, start-ups have brilliant ideas. As the founder, you have to start your ascent somewhere. Your brilliant ideas must have a map to become a reality. The terrain of that map is rough. Not everybody has the luxury of life and funding afforded to people like Bill Gates. Most founders are raised in rough conditions that create hunger. This struggle can be used as a force for good and resilient determination.

Why is base camp important for mountain climbers? Because this is where you take stock and prepare. Scaling is all about preparation—tactically, emotionally, physically. There is an acclimation process where you must adapt to a decrease in the partial pressure of oxygen (quick bio lesson: our lungs depend on pressure gradient to move oxygen through the air sacs). Less oxygen pressure as you reach higher altitudes feels like less oxygen or less air, but that is not actually true. In addition to the whole gasping for breath as you climb, your body also has to acclimate to new temperatures and a myriad of unexpected situations yet to unfold.

When you climb a mountain at a high altitude, you can't go straight to the summit. Sometimes you have to go back to the base camp after reaching each summit. This process is called "acclimation."

Building a business requires you to acclimate, too. Sometimes you have to take a few steps back in order to move forward. Finding that "Summit" to take a break and reverse back to the Base Camp to acclimate at the right time is so critical. Sometimes, your business boomed because of serendipity. It could create a false reality that you can go straight to the top without acclimation. This is one of the reasons many start-ups' growth stalled once they hit the $50 million mark.

Taking a step back to reevaluate your goals and adjust your strategy and execution plan is a must. Reflect, learn, and think about what you would do differently. Listen to others. If I did not listen to my guide, I would not have been successful. I followed those instructions to a T. Your guides in business are the people you hire beyond the founding team. They are experienced in the practical—they've been there, done that already. These may not be the people you grew up with.

What founders feel at this stage: exhausted, thrilled, fearful.

A successful founder also understands whom to listen to and what specific commentary is most important to take note of from their executive team. The art of listening is perhaps one of the most important skills a founder can develop. Taking the time to understand what is really being said and turning that into execution is a critical competency that many start-up founders fall short on for various reasons: ego, lack of practice or empathy, or simply not realizing the importance of hearing other views.

So, here we are. Base Camp is a profound marker that reminds us that preparation is so important when success or adversity is triggered because you then know how to react and move forward.

Scaling a start-up is a marathon, not a sprint. This book will explore 26 micro-decisions that must be made along the way in order to scale without sacrificing yourself, the people you love, and the company you are passionate about. Let's explore the first micro-decision together.

Decision #1: Why Are You on This Journey?

What is my "why"? What is the problem I am solving? Am I doing what I'm supposed to be doing with my life and with my business? These are soul-searching questions most of us are wise to explore. You, as a start-up founder, will probably ask them more than once.

Simon Sinek made that little three-letter word: "why" famous. His TED talk about the golden circles and how "why" should be the lead question a person or company explores has been watched more than 50 million times. Why is this one of the most-watched TED talks of all time? Because knowing your why is the hub by which we strike our path. Not every company wants to be an Apple, nor should every start-up compare themselves with Amazon or Google. For some, exiting after reaching the first or second peak might be their choice.

Your peak is self-defined and ties back to your purpose. One person's peak is different from another's. Think about it, when Amazon founder Jeff Bezos started his bookstore, he didn't see where he would be today. Yet, he was the first person to reach a net worth of $200 billion.[1]

---

[1]Annie Palmer, "Jeff Bezos is now worth more than $200 billion," CNBC, Published August 26, 2020, https://www.cnbc.com/2020/08/26/amazon-ceo-jeff -bezos-worth-more-than-200-billion.html

Peak is defined as this: What would you like to be remembered for as a person? When a person goes to a funeral, no one talks about the business they were in. You remember how that person made you feel based on what you experienced together or how they supported you or how they helped you through challenging times. What legacy do you want to leave behind? How do you want to be remembered?

Making Grandma proud, spreading her ashes on a tall mountain was a "peak" for me. Early in my career, I thought staying special and creating a legacy meant working twice as hard as anyone else. Working hard is important, but working hard does not create a legacy. No statues are built for the hardest worker in the minds of people. A decade later, making a positive impact is how I stay special.

The amount of impact we make is optional. Jeff Bezos can have $200 billion, but what he does with it is up to him.

My idols are Bill and Melinda Gates because of the money they've given to education, to women in technology. They devoted half their lives—lives beyond their careers—to serve the broader world and the underrepresented. This is how they will be remembered.

When we know our "why," we know our purpose on a broad scale. In all of my contributions to helping major tech companies reach greater levels of success, I now realize my "why" has long been rooted in being a multiplier—someone who multiplies other people's success.

When we know our "why" behind starting a company, we know the purpose behind the endeavor. The "why" behind ascending Mount Everest was to keep a sacred promise to my grandmother. I felt unstoppable. I made up my mind that nothing would hold me back from my climb. My destination started out not on any map, but in my mind. It started out as a dream …

Consider *your* dreams. You are a founder. You are busy. Your runway is short, the staff is skeletal, if that. You run lean and mean. There are a thousand ways this can go, a thousand actions you can take right now. You don't know the path, but you sure know the packing list for the journey: pitch deck for investors, exit strategy outline, elevator speech, job descriptions and hiring practices, meetings with current investors, business plan revisions (do these ever end?), product roadmap, marketing strategy, product launch strategy, delegation … the list goes on forever. So, how do you know you're investing time in the right places and on the right things so your start-up takes root? Is taking time to step back and dream important?

Without question, the answer is yes.

As I've mentioned, many people say a business is "your baby." I tend to look at it more as a dream, a North Star that you haven't yet reached but which is completely reachable if you align vision with strategy and execution and cure your disconnects. Return to your North Star again and again. The reason you set out on this journey will not change—but your vision and/or strategy might. So, be prepared. Most companies have a set of strategies for their revenue target, growth strategy/drivers, or go-to-market, but there might not be the right processes to follow. You might see other emerging markets and opportunities.

Our friends from Jebbit pivoted from a marketing company to a first-party data company, and their execution plan is much different when evaluating market assumptions. Jebbit needed to broaden distribution channels through key partnerships with Marketo, Adobe, Hubspot, and Salesforce. Their "why" never changed, but their strategy evolved, ultimately positioning Jebbit as an extension of much larger companies and dramatically improving marketing conversion.

Decision #2: What Problems Are You Solving?

If I had to pick the most important question along your journey, this would be the winner.

What real problems are you solving? To whom do these problems matter? Does anyone else solve the same problem? What differentiates you? Do people care about the problems you are trying to solve? Why do they care? Why are you chosen as THE solution provider to that problem? Are you solving a problem the world cares about, or a problem YOU alone care about?

UX designer Sarah Doody writes in The UX Notebook newsletter, "If you can't define the problem, then don't design a solution."

"Fall in love with a problem, not a specific solution," says Laura Javier, a product designer at Instagram and Facebook. This critical decision is where you need to do some serious research as to whether the problem you are trying to solve has an impact on certain types of businesses, how big the address-able market is, and who else is already doing it.

When you dive into the problem, you explore the impact you are making with your product. Be obsessively passionate about *discovering* the problem. When you solve for X, what is the equation's outcome? It may seem small to others, but it's critical for you to have the drive and insight to move forward and create beyond the product at face value.

You must articulate the problem you are solving and bring others with you.

For example, I worked with an AI company that had ten people, including four co-founders. I asked them this question: "Why did you start the company?" They tried to solve the problem of people who wanted to keep track of financials, the type of people who would ask: "How much did our family spend on our trip to see the big mouse? What's the cost of that bachelorette party to Nashville?" You could add up the credit cards, cash, debit cards, Venmo and PayPal payments manually, sure, but *will you* take the time to do that? Not likely. So, my client developed a voice-activated app that would understand your expenses through conversation. It was pretty cool. You could tell the app what you wanted to do and how much the idea cost, and the app would then figure out your financial status and determine if you could afford a side excursion or expensive meal.

This app does solve a problem, but does it solve THE problem? What was lacking was that the problem was not a problem for everybody. So, we dug into that. Naturally, I started by asking questions (don't fall out of your chair in shock):

- What about people who don't have bank accounts?
- What about people who can't afford traveling?
- What about people who care less about personal finance?
- What unique problem does your solution solve?

We went beyond financial purposes because that is not the daily struggle. The solution was unique because of its deep learning solution that understands human conversations. That means the solution could potentially offer in-car voice assistance or enhance drive-through orders for quick-service restaurants. We turned it from a $170,000 a year business to a $4.5 million company. We did it by analyzing the problem because the most important part of this multifaceted question is your audience, or your Ideal Customer Profile (ICP).

How do you segment your ICP? Here are several ways to do it:

- By use cases
- Enterprise vs. SMB vs. Mid-Market
- Industry vertical
- Geographic market
- Buyer persona
- User persona

Figuring out the problem you must solve sounds simple, but there is much work to be done. Sit with the problem, analyze it, and talk to your audience about it.

Then, feel that rush of confidence like the whipping winds of Mount Everest. You just traversed a pivotal, game-changing juncture.

Decision #3: What Does Success Look Like to You?

Is success conquering the Summit? Scaling your company to become a Unicorn? Going public? Define your North Star, knowing that your North Star could evolve.

Many founders focus so much on the product that they don't have time to connect with others. Sixteen-hour days where lunch is a luxury are common. That's not sustainable. And it's short-sighted.

To be strategic, you have to make mind space for yourself, to carve out one or two hours a day to think. You can see the trees, but not the forest otherwise. Spending time away from the day-to-day business unleashes my brainpower. Here is where you begin to choreograph your start-up's graceful climb.

As a founder, focus on defining your North Star, articulating that to your team. The ability to empower experienced leaders and determine when to step in sets successful companies apart from others.

That was why Marketo was successful. The co-founder and CEO Phil Fernandez not only defined the North Star, but also took time to articulate what it means to each department and translate it into actionable OKRs (Objectives and Key Results).

Have a higher goal than just focusing on your company. Because if you don't make it to the Summit the first time, you can try it again with the lessons learned.

We've all seen start-ups crash and burn. It's easy to lose sight of the runway when you feel you are making history.

So, when you're thinking about success, factor in the "ordinary." Not all solutions turn into gazillion-dollar front-page headlines. Changing the world is noble, and it's thrilling to imagine yourself on the cover of Fast Company magazine; however, selling bottled water (or a simple app to figure expenses) is just as important as developing robots that dance the Cha Cha Slide.

Scaling the tech start-up mountain goes beyond innovating, creating, pitching, and selling. Those are exciting things, to be sure, but there are mundane tasks you must also do. Consider where we are: Base Camp. There's that all-important word: "basic."

Scaling your company is physically and mentally demanding. Like any accomplished athlete, you must train, prepare, and get the basics down. The basics of mountain climbing require you to learn, ask questions, go over your equipment list a hundred times, test your gear, rest, review the map, line up your guides, get to know the people you will climb with so you trust them and they trust you, and more.

You can point to just about any accomplished person and see how they embrace the ordinary. Cellist Yo-Yo Ma estimates that he practices 10,000 hours every 5 years, or 5 to 6 hours per day[1]. This includes scales—the same ones he did as a child—so his muscle memory is flawless. This doesn't include the time he is *thinking* about his beautiful cello or his exploration into new sounds and new ways to connect with

---

[1] Alec Nevala Lee, "The 50,000 Hours of Yo-Yo Ma," nevalalee.wordpress.com, published May 8, 2021, https://nevalalee.wordpress.com/2012/05/08/the-50000-hours-of-yo-yo-ma.

audiences. Taking this a step further, why do you think he's so loved for his performances and music? I contend it comes down to one thing: because he loves the music he makes with his cello. He pays attention to the basics so he can create the extraordinary.

Once again, we see the start-up founder's decisions are not mutually exclusive of one another. They are a complex, inter-related web strengthened by your center. Again, your "why" as a founder continues to influence your climb. I've heard that if you lose your why, you lose your way. The right path isn't always glamorous. Oftentimes, though, big strides are made in the most ordinary ways.

Decision #4: How Will You Honor Your Brand?

Book the big conference room. Gather your team. Call a brand meeting. After everyone sits down, leave an empty chair.

That seat is where your brand gets to sit.

In the Chinese culture, honoring parents and clan elders goes back thousands of years. Those who come before us have wisdom. They are our roots. They fuel our legacy.

Your brand came before you started the company, probably before you thought of that cool tech idea. Your brand comes from inside you, its founder. Your brand is your values, core beliefs, higher mission, an expression of your "why."

You are a product creator now. You are also a brand creator.

As early as possible, consider how you're going to extend the impact your brand creates and include others in how you articulate that message in the branding so you are successful longer-term. This is a foundation for building any company. Brand deserves your attention, major thinking time, and love because, after all, your brand is how others outside your organization perceive you. You don't want this very important fact to be the stumbling block to scaling.

Dig deep to find your vision and mission. Explore the why/what/how you got there, the anticipated risk, and how you measure success. For the start-up launching the expense app, these questions solidified the MVP. We didn't just hit a set of numbers, we *pursued* them with a vengeance.

In all my conversations with start-up founders, branding is like a vast open sea where the waves rise and fall without the sailor having any bearing on which direction they are going. Founders are tech wizards, so they quail at the mere thought that they could possibly master their brand. After all, there are dozens of so-called essential brand statements. YFS Magazine is for seed, start-up, and growth companies. In one article, it cited 14 different brand terms[1]:

- Brand
- Brand architecture
- Brand promise
- Brand equity
- Brand experience

---

[1] 14 Branding Terms Every Entrepreneur Should know, Yes Magazine, Published Jan 19, 2015, https://yfsmagazine.com/2015/01/19/14-branding-terms-every-entrepreneur-should-know/

- Brand extension
- Brand identity
- Brand image
- Brand licensing
- Brand personality
- Brand strategy
- Co-branding
- Rebranding
- Repositioning
- Visual identity

Additionally, I'd say there are three more terms: brand essence, brand pillars, and brand presence. There's probably a longer list if we really sat around the campfire and thought about it.

No wonder you want to get back to coding and put your brand on a shelf!

Let me take a weight off your shoulders and offer you a brand-new viewpoint (sorry, couldn't resist!). There are no right answers. There are only true answers. It's complicated when the imposter syndrome voice inside you sassily points out you're not a brand expert. Enough already.

Let's take a little tech start-up that launched on April 12, 1991, for example. You may have heard of them. Today, that start-up Salesforce has 30,000 employees globally and more than $17 billion in revenues as of Q4 2020.[1] According to a

---

[1]Salesforce, Salesforce Announces Record Fourth Quarter and Full Year Fiscal 2020 Results, Salesforce.com, published February 25, 2020, https://investor .salesforce.com/press-releases/press-release-details/2020/Salesforce-Announces -Record-Fourth-Quarter-and-Full-Year-Fiscal-2020-Results/default.aspx

blog by Visible, Salesforce founder Marc Benioff said, "While a company is growing fast, there is nothing more important than constant communication and complete alignment. We've been able to achieve both with the help of a secret management process that I developed a number of years ago."[1]

The process Benioff is referring to is V2MOM, and it combines brand, strategy, and measurement in a short, concise format. V2MOM is powerful. I've used it many times in advising start-ups to Fortune 500 companies. Here it is:

- VISION (make the future resonate)
- VALUES (identify core beliefs)
- METHODS (build your path)
- OBSTACLES (anticipate risk)
- MEASURES (track results)

What I love about V2MOM is its simplicity. (Besides, if it's good enough for Marc Benioff, it's good enough for the rest of us!) These five points inform your market focus, the customers you seek, and those you don't. They paint a picture of the world you hope to create. They stipulate the agreed-upon norms. Let's dismantle V2MOM and see what it's made of.

Vision. Vision clarifies what mission accomplished looks like and how the world has changed. It defines your future history. For example, *Embrace A Digitally Connected Go-To-Customer Strategy and Deliver Meaningful Experience to Buyers.*

---

[1]Mark Benioff, "Create strategic company alignment with V2MOM", The 360 blog on salesforce.com, published May 1, 2020, https://www.salesforce.com/blog/how-to-create-alignment-within-your-company/ /

Values. Values express the core truth of your aspirational culture. They vitalize the organization as a rallying cry and make critical decisions 10 times easier. Here are some examples:

> Clarity: Customer obsessed (internal and external customers)
> Direct: Journey aware (clearly defined cross-functional roles and responsibilities along customer journey)
> Expect: Engagement-driven (it is critical to engage with your customers)
> Inspire: Personalized (tailored approach based on evolving needs)

According to Trailhead, Salesforce's learning arm: "The very first V2MOM at Salesforce included Values like 'world class organization,' 'time to market,' and 'usability.' Now, our business Values includes words like 'trust,' 'customer success,' and 'innovation.'"

Methods. Methods are the "how." What actions must you take to achieve your vision?

Obstacles. Obstacles are the anticipated risks. Imagining your start-up journey as a tall mountain with slippery slopes, you know you need to prepare for the unexpected. Ask: What will make your journey harder, and what stands in the way of your company's success?

Measures. Metrics are how you will measure the outcome of your methods. These are specific and are oftentimes number-driven.

You might be wondering: What about my mission statement? While there's some debate about this, a great mission statement runs in step with your "why." A mission statement is an inward- and outward-facing declaration that clarifies what you do, for whom, and why.

Here's Jebbit's mission statement:

Our mission is to make every experience assumption free by asking people explicitly and directly about their interests, motivations, and preferences.[1]

Your brand—in three words. People do business with those companies that have shared value. In order to extend your business, your brand reputation precedes you.

When I work with founders, I ask them to describe the impact of their company to me in three words. This seems to be the most challenging question for them. Not only are there inconsistent views among co-founders, but it inevitably points out the lack of a well-thought-out branding strategy.

Branding is one of those elusive topics that conjures up the thought of expensive brand consultancies with ping-pong tables and a fully stocked bar for Friday revelry. Look inward. This is *your* company. Your brand is one of your most valuable assets. Identify your brand identity in three words: what you do, for whom, and why. Product fit and competitive positioning depend on it.

---

[1] Jebbit Marketing, Meet Jebbit – Redefining How the World Think About Data, "Our Story", Jebbit.com, https://www.jebbit.com/about

Building your brand identity into the product early on sets a successful company apart. It is the connection between your brand and how people will "see" your brand.

How do you want to be perceived? How do you want to be remembered?

For the conversational AI company I advised, people could go to the app and ask about financial balances and information. We learned about the challenges people have with timely interaction, and we found out that it was not just banking that the app could revolutionize, but conversations as people are driving. They might say: "I'm on my way to New York. How much gas do I have?" Or, as you drive through a fast-food line, the app can help you make the experience more seamless. As we went through the process, we discovered we weren't limited. We dug deep into what drove the "why" of the founder, how it mattered to others, and customer segmentation. Then, we identified the three words to express the brand: revolutionize the conversations.

The results were astounding. We realized that the solution was not only a good fit for financial service companies, it solved problems for other industries that needed to improve their voice-activated customer services like QSR (Quick Service Restaurant) drive-through ordering systems and in-car voice-activated assistant systems.

You are an extension of your brand. Customers are oftentimes not just buying the brand, they are buying you. You can make an impact in the community and focus on other things outside the company to show the positive side of you as a person and your brand. Many founders gravitate to solutions.

Yet, take a page from the younger generation. Their average screen time is four hours per day. They are online and digital. Even if you are selling B2B, you are still selling to humans, which makes all sales H2H, or human to human. There's a reason why some brands are very much loved: they build attachment. Gainsight CEO Nick Mehta leads a customer success software company that, according to a company press release, achieved 361% year-over-year growth for its product experience platform Gainsight PX at the close of its fiscal year in 2020.[1] Is the company superior? Not really. But people love Nick. Everybody knows him in the customer experience field. Oftentimes, people buy the product *because* of Nick. How do people get to know him?

Nick is active on Twitter and LinkedIn and speaks regularly at conferences. He does not talk about himself much. Rather, he talks about empathy and issues that impact humanity. He is a founder with high emotional intelligence (plus, he's just a great person to be around!). Nick is a magnate, and he proves the law of reciprocity because he gives and shares and inspires others to want to give and share back to him and his company. People trust him.

He holds a conference called Pulse in New York, and invited me as a guest speaker one year. The topic was "Is the Chief Customer Officer a pathway to becoming CEO?" I enjoyed speaking with him because he has a very dynamic

---

[1]Gainsight News, "Gainsight Highlights Year Of Record Growth; Ends Fiscal Year with Record-Breaking Quarter for Gainsight PX," Gainsight press release, Gainsight.com, Published February 26, 2020, https://www.gainsight.com/press /release/gainsight-highlights-year-of-record-growth-ends-fiscal-year-with-record -breaking-quarter-for-gainsight-px/

personality and understands customer success really well, a rarity among CEOs.

There are many things that Gainsight does well, and one of them is its founder's engagement with others. Your social media presence, involvement in the community and industry, and relationships with others matter, not just for customer success, but for long-term success. It certainly has influenced Gainsight's perception and value in the marketplace.

By the close of 2020, Gainsight sold to Vista for $1.1 billion.[1]

Decision #5: How Will You Prepare for The Climb?

No matter how prepared you are, you will always run into unexpected situations. I'm not trying to be defeatist because I believe preparation has saved many from disaster, myself included, but give yourself permission to not be perfect. The start-up world is a minefield. That's a given. There will be things out of your control, like a key employee leaving the team or a global pandemic, or a sudden shift in consumer buying behavior. Think of preparedness like cybersecurity— how you respond to an event is predicated on your response framework.

---

[1]Ron Miller, Alex Wilhelm,"Vista acquires Gainsight for $1.1B, adding to its growing enterprise arsenal," Tech Crunch, Published November 30, 2020, https://techcrunch.com/2020/11/30/vista-acquires-gainsight-for-1-1b -adding-to-its-growing-enterprise-arsenal/

For example, it is perilous and foolish to get wet at a high elevation. You could lose fingers or toes in a matter of minutes. This is about being prepared. Many founders run into situations they didn't even know would happen. This is why we begin at Base Camp and methodically go up the mountain. Here are a few things to get you thinking:

- Are you keeping your "why" of starting the company in your line of sight?
- What is your V2MOM (Vision, Value, Methods, Obstacles, Measurement)?
- Who is on your minimum viable team to carry out your mission?
- Who are the strategic resources you need to retain or hire to create capabilities you don't have but need to have?

Before I head out for any adventure, I try to understand the risk associated with the adventure first, close all the doors and windows of my home, and forward the mail before I leave. What does this mean to your business? It means to assess all the risks from a strategy, execution, and team perspective and come up with a mitigation plan prior to climbing to the next Summit. The risks you ran into in the past might be different from those you are going to experience next. People you grew up with might not be the right business partners as you set out to climb higher. The ability to separate your personal attachment from business decisions is a must for successful founders. Founders are oftentimes so tied to their original ideas that they can't adapt when things go south. That's when it is time to pivot or redirect and bring someone else in who can lead the effort.

Remember Tom and Jonathan? In 2011, there were one hundred MarTech companies. Five years later, there were 7,000. No way could they have seen that coming. But that was OK because they were prepared to deal with it. Is it time for you to pivot and stand out?

Onward

I was the only one by my grandmother's side right before she passed away. When she gave me her last three wishes—to stay special, make the world proud, and spread her ashes on a tall mountain—she also gave me a puzzle to decode.

My cousins and I asked ourselves: What is a tall mountain? Which one do we choose? How will we know if it is tall by her definition?

When you are not sure, it is good to go where there is no cause for misunderstanding; where the answer is clearly right in front of you. Everest took all doubt away. I had my mission. I knew what to do. I knew why I was doing it.

Proceed with purpose and intention. Make your path. Tame the mountain.

Chapter 2

TURN IDEA INTO PRODUCT CAMP

Along my expedition up Mount Everest, there were many situations that were impossible to anticipate. Any climb up that majestic mountain, a 29,032-foot pile of rock, is enveloped in constant change. There's the weather, your health, the health of your team, the condition of your gear, and other teams moving all around you. How you face those changing conditions starts long before you start your expedition.

Where you come from—all your past experiences, history, and life lessons—shapes how you forge the path.

Because my parents were diplomats, they spent a lot of time overseas, only coming home every other year for one month. As a result, I was raised by my grandmother, the woman who would later lead me to my trek up Everest. She never went to school, but taught herself to read. She was self-taught, self-made, and the best role model I could ever hope for.

I grew up with eight noisy, always hungry, rambunctious cousins, children from my mother's four siblings, plus my brother. The Big Nine. We could have been a Chinese version of the von Trapp family from the "Sound of Music"—except we had no grand mansion, no servants or sumptuous gardens to roam in (or the voices to sing with!). I was the youngest and only girl. Life, for me, was growing up as a survivor.

Memories flood my senses as I climb. Eating fast when the dish of food was placed on the wooden kitchen table. Wearing boy's clothes until I was 10. Sleeping in a bed with a half-dozen other children who were just as hungry as I was. Being a girl or, perhaps more accurately, not being a boy, meant I was regarded as the least important human being in almost everyone's eyes. Grandma was the exception. She saw something in me.

No matter for the things we lacked, we always felt loved by my grandmother.

Listening to Grandma's stories during bedtime was magical. There was a moral imperative in every tale she told. Some people see the world through stories, and when they share them, your small world suddenly becomes magnanimous. Grandma's stories always had a moral lesson. I was the one who listened the best, my knees gathered up in my arms, hanging on her every word. I could recite each story as though they were imprinted upon my mind. Grandma wanted me to grow up strong. If being strong was being like her, I wanted that, too.

Grandma taught me to be a straight shooter, perseverant as well as hardworking, always putting other people's concerns ahead of my own.

Her wisdom drives me forward, up the mountain, even though I want to quit, turn back and give up. Something inside me triggers Grandma's stories, the ones about how we are not just individuals, but part of something much larger than ourselves.

My ascent is not just about me.

Temperature changes drastically throughout the day. At base camp, I put on jeans and a T-shirt. I add a sweater. I am warm. I am cold. I am not sure of what I feel anymore. At night, I lay on a bed made of wood in a barren cabin. No, nighttime is like the room in *Goodnight Moon* where the rabbit has all of 10 items around him. Climbing is about less. Climbing is about the bare minimum. There is no sleeping bag; we sleep in our ski outfit. We paid a lot for just a blanket. You never know how much you miss nuzzling your face into a soft, cotton throw with the smell of spring from your favorite brand of dryer sheet. Here, the only smell is a mix of rotting paper and sweat.

Before we even begin the climb, the Canon camera I bought for the trip crashes to the floor. My heart shatters as I hear the hard thwack of metal on wood. We take out the memory card in the hopes of finding another person along the way with the same camera body. Fate does not disappoint. A woman from Singapore lends me her camera body. I attach my telephoto zoom lens, something she does not have. We are grateful to find each other on this journey.

No one can leave the room at night. If you go to the bathroom at night, you use the bowl in your room. "Cool temperatures mean that your body will have to divert some of its oxygen simply to keep you warm. On average, ambient temperature falls about 4°F for each 1,000 feet of elevation"[1].

---

[1] "Into thin air: Medical problems at new heights," Harvard Health Publishing, Published March 2014, https://www.health.harvard.edu/newsletter_article /Into_thin_air_Medical_problems_at_new_heights

We moderate what we eat and drink. My body reacts to the elevation. I am dizzy. I have diarrhea, a common high-altitude reaction. Imagine having to find a place to "go," then let everyone in your group know about it. If I drank water, I would get it, and you can't survive without water, so …

I am beginning to break down, to not function normally. I am suffering.

Not everyone feels this way. I am joined on the trip by people who know me well, like Doris, one of my best friends from middle school. The first day I arrive, I react so badly that I have to go to bed when we reach 12,000 feet. My body begs for rest. Doris feels nothing. Instead, she goes to the local gift shops. *She is so much BETTER than me,* I whisper to myself before I fall asleep.

Or so I thought.

After we pass the third night, she tells me she cannot go on. She drops. They keep taking people away who, if they continued, would not be physically able to make it back down the mountain. It is too risky for them to forge ahead. One by one, they go.

Because I am the first one to react badly, I think I am the weakest, but I realize this is not true. When you have the heart and mind to overcome a challenge, you endure.

Turn Idea into Product Camp

The desire to abandon the climb happens with all of us from time to time. Going from idea to product puts you at a crossroad. There are days you make no progress. You look around, and there are zero customers in sight. Investors won't return your phone calls. No money is coming in. You hit the wall, and you are not sure how to overcome that challenge. On your worst days, you dream of working for someone else; a desk job in a place where somebody else worries about keeping the lights on.

Maybe you are a perfectionist. Most founders I've counseled strive for *being perfect*, particularly during the Turn Idea into Product Camp. Why is this? Because they focus on product building.

Step out of that zone. Listen to others. Like a hike up Mount Everest, carry with you the bare essentials. There is a role for perfectionism, but it isn't about you being flawless—it is about creating the perfect, minimally viable product.

Eric Ries, author of the book *The Lean Startup*, puts it this way: "As you consider building your own minimum viable product, let this simple rule suffice: remove any feature, process, or effort that does not contribute directly to the learning you seek."[1]

Minimal Viable Product (MVP) is defined as a product with only a basic set of features—just enough to capture the attention of early adopters and make your solution unique. According to Forbes, the advantages of an MVP include getting to market in the shortest amount of time, product testing before a full release of the product, minimizing costly capital expenses, providing insight, and building your user base early on. The article goes on to say: "In chase of the perfect product, some companies lose their focus on the core value

---

[1]Eric Ries, *The Lean Startup: How Today's Entrepreneurs Use Continuous Innovation to Create Radically Successful Businesses*, Crown Business, Published in 2011, http://theleanstartup.com/

and try to include every single feature. An MVP becomes overloaded with features, a company loses its money and fails to succeed."[1]

If you build your product without a broader view, you could be off. This is called the Minimum Viable Repeatability Disconnect. This is when you need to have an experienced Sherpa to guide you.

After all, who wants to wallow in all that suffering for nothing?

Decision #6: What is Your Minimal Viable Product (MVP)?

To be at least minimally viable, a product must be marketable—not evidence of technical prowess too impractical to sell. But how do you nail marketability? Explain the problem you are solving as well as your product.

What founders feel at this stage: excited! You are anxious to turn your idea into a real product.

By now, you've already deeply explored the fundamental problem you are solving. Next, you must align your brand, customer segmentation, team, and resource skill set to transform your idea into an MVP.

---

[1] Julia Tokariva, "What is a Minimal Viable Product and Why Do Companies Need Them?" Forbes, Published February 27, 2018, https://www.forbes.com /sites/quora/2018/02/27/what-is-a-minimum-viable-product-and-why-do -companies-need-them/?sh=6f2f1275382c

Explore:

- Who cares about the problem you are trying to solve?
- Is there anyone else solving the same problem?
- What type of team do you need to have in place to achieve your vision?

While the Turn Idea into Product Camp is messy, tiring, and emotional, an MVP keeps you moving in the right direction more fearlessly and with a greater sense of purpose. Here, you're not focused on just features and functionalities of your product; you're diving into the use case for that product and positioning your product as a well-defined and relevant customer solution that ultimately will become scalable.

Decision #7: How Will You Pilot Your Product?

Think like a scientist armed with a hypothesis of how your product will solve the problem and create a go-to-market business model from there. Test the idea with two or three potential customers. Articulate a use case to a beta customer who is in your Ideal Customer Profile. Within the ICP, focus on one use case at a time and the specific issues for each.

Conducting pilots validates your thinking and gauges how effective your solution will be. Share your pilot with your team; lean on them to help get funding from investors to launch pilots and use insight to refine your MVP. Your work on this now will accelerate scaling and give you the peace of mind to move forward more fearlessly.

Avoid boiling the ocean. Start with a small pilot. The user experience needs to be very simple. Is the capability of the product easy for customers to adopt? What is the business outcome for customers? What is the required capability for the solution? How will you measure that? What are the minimum viable solutions your product must have? Map these answers to a list of features. Can you build that with what you have? Do you have the team to do it? When you build your MVP, is the customer ready to buy or do you need a customer to invest in you and build together? Is there any other alternative problem you can solve in a faster manner with fewer resources involved? Is time-to-value mission critical to your ICP? How much time does it take them to solve the problem today? How much pain are they in? What is the business impact of this pain? How would they solve the problem if you didn't exist? How big is the barrier to entry (the cost to enter a market)? The bigger the barrier to entry, the stickier your solution is. Validate your assumptions.

Think iterative. Don't go too deep until you have the basic product already, and then, and only then, invest in additional features and expansive capabilities.

Onward

Taking a product to market is not just about the product. Many people have asked me if I journaled through my ascent of Mount Everest. That is impossible. You cannot write when you are suffering. Pretending you're Hemingway is a lost cause. Surviving, moving forward, following your guides' advice, checking your gear, recognizing less is more, thinking about what is good for the team as a whole, taking strength from your core beliefs, communicating with your group, remembering your "why" ... these are the basic things you focus on as you ascend, and these are the decisions a founder must face when they spend time in the Turn Idea into Product Camp.

Chapter 3

MOVE PRODUCT
TO MARKET CAMP

I had taken the train from Beijing to Lhasa. As a U.S. citizen, you cannot visit there without a permit, and you are not allowed to go alone without a certified Sherpa and driver. I selected mine based on their experience and other people's recommendation, but real experience does not show its hand until you see it in action.

The entry point at the bottom of the mountain is for tourists, not professional climbers. There were many climbers the day we arrived. There was no proper road to get us to ground zero. Many cars were sidelined with flat tires because of the jagged terrain. When our car's tires caught the sharp edge of the mountain, our driver had a spare and changed it quickly for us. My trip was the fifth one of the year for him. Most climbers will go in April, May, or June, but we went during the off-season in July.

Our Sherpa, Hassan, was one of the best. If I ever go there again, he's the one I want by my side. We paid the locals who blocked the road so we could get by. Hassan had a stack of thin, paper one-yuan notes (one RMB in Chinese currency is equivalent to about 15 cents in U.S. currency). I thought to myself, *this guy really knows how to get by.* If it were just me, I wouldn't have been able to go forward. The narrow dirt road was treacherous. We stopped at a few local residences along the way to eat—luckily, Hassan knew the people who would cook for us. He knew who to trust. If you don't know people, you are stuck. Hassan turned what could have been a horrible experience into a pleasant one. We took photos along the way, and I gave the little kids candy. One grandpa shared with me that he was surprised I gave them chocolate. I would have done much more had I known the poverty and needs of the people who fed off the generosity of strangers.

I do not know how long I will last. I have no choice. I am carrying my grandmother's ashes, and I have no way back. I have to move forward in the leanest, meanest, bare-minimum way I can. I am not looking for glory or prepping for a glamorous photoshoot. I don't care about shopping, snapping photographs, calling home, or writing letters. I don't see anything but the purpose of our trip. At nightfall, I collapse into the bed. There are no smartphones. My little alarm clock wakes me up on time.

Hassan, our Sherpa and driver, gives instructions, and I follow them. Just like the stories Grandma told me, I listen to every word. I imprint Hassan's advice on my heart. I put my life in the hands of my guides and follow along with everything they tell me. I trust. I listen. I ask questions. And, at the end of each day, we spend time planning for the next.

Move Product to Market Camp

In the start-up world, the route to the top is lonely. Few people may understand what you are truly experiencing as a founder. Others may be by your side, but few understand how you *feel*.

Adapting to the changing environment along the way is now mandatory as you ascend to the Move Product to Market camp. At this stage, there are always unexpected events where you don't have all the facts you need to move forward. You run into things you never experienced before. Sometimes, you cannot take the time to wait and undergo a full decision process. However, you have laid a good foundation by examining the problems your product solves, exploring your brand, and building a minimal viable product that is spot-on.

You'll find in the Move Product to Market Camp it is challenging to strike a balance. Sometimes you don't know if you have the right Sherpa beside you. Did I know I had the right guide before my climb? No. I found out that afterward. Multiple people recommended him, but the true test is what you experience with a person. As a founder or an executive, you don't see failure until you crash. Many companies grow because of momentum. With rapid success, founders sometimes are tempted to stop listening and appreciating experienced people. The business continues but can't scale at the speed it is capable of. Once you grow to $50 million, you may stall, not realizing you could actually scale to $200 million the next three years. Like a whiteout on a mountainside, you simply may not have clear visibility ahead.

As you move from product to market, if you are a tech founder without any experience building a company, this is where you need to find an experienced Sherpa to guide you. Here is when you start raising more funds. Usually, this is the most difficult time of the climb—but you are brave! Invite naysayers and dissenters; surround yourself with experienced people. Moving product to market is a precarious, slippery slope and the most likely camp to bring a company down.

Decision #8: What Product Category Are You REALLY In?

Does the category you have placed your product in already exist? Is that product category innovative and relevant to the current market environment? Are you solving a problem everyone in *this* particular category cares about?

The higher impact it has within a category, the more graceful your climb. A gap left behind by being in the wrong product category is a massive disconnect for start-ups because they are so internally focused on product development. Instead, look up. See the next focal point on your journey and keep climbing toward not just building your product but creating a whole new category in the industry.

What founders feel at this stage: vulnerable.

In order to create a category or become a leader in an existing category, you need to understand the market, customer segmentation, competitive landscape, distribution channels, market trends, and where your solution fits in.

Nike does not sell shoes; it sells inspiration. Nike sells the promise you can be a top performer because the brand supports athletes who take action in achieving their goals. In a $24.2 billion industry, Nike still ranks number one. Before it got there, though, the company had to be number one in people's minds and hearts. Buyers don't buy into the color and construction of the shoes, but rather how the shoe makes them feel.

Another example of a company I was fortunate to have a front-row seat with is Adobe. As of this writing, this $11 billion software company is known as the one that created (and still owns) the digital marketing category. I joined the company when it was pivoting to own the category. What I learned was astounding. The secret source of Adobe's success was its ability to create an active listening path to customers.

Microsoft was an early adopter of Adobe Digital Marketing solution. Brad Rancher, head of engineering at the time, and I visited Microsoft on a monthly basis. We listened. We translated their feedback into a product roadmap. We adjusted the go-to-market strategy and service offerings. We improved significantly.

In order to scale faster and more fearlessly, you must think big. Think *category*. What is the minimal viable category you are entering? Is it insurer tech, health tech, marketing tech, AI, or a new category altogether?

Decision #9: Who Will Be By Your Side, and Who Will Leave?

As a founder, having someone you trust by your side may not be enough to gain traction. This is a real challenge. One way to move past this challenge and scale the tech start-up mountain more fearlessly is to clearly define your vision and goal, then find someone who has already done so and can operationalize your vision by your side (we'll talk more on this in chapter seven!). Fact: You cannot do everything alone. By leaning on someone with complementary expertise, you ascend to the next level while believing this person will take you further.

It takes four different types of leaders with different skill sets to formulate a minimum viable team to scale. They are:

> **Thought Leader:** a leader who envisions something that does not yet exist.
> **Challenger:** a leader who challenges whether the new idea has value for stakeholders.
> **Collaborator:** a leader who brings different people from across the organization together.
> **Operator:** a leader who carries out execution with predictable and sustainable results.

It is paramount to clarify who plays what role, help everyone to understand why you are on this journey together, and articulate why it matters to *everyone* in the same way it matters to your organization.

The mistake founders make after raising money is hiring friends and family, or the top 10% of people they know. You don't know what you will come across while building a company. As you head into a new market, you must have people with that specialized knowledge to help you. Build your team beyond your network, hire those top 1% in the industry and those who deliver and have shared values, beliefs and care about customers and team. Additionally, think about how you will *empower them to succeed.*

As a start-up founder, you will run into unique experiences you could never have imagined. When you are in it, you need a Sherpa who has been there, done that so you know what to anticipate.

Not Everyone in a Start-up Makes the Ascent

Sometimes, the people who begin the start-up journey don't stay with you—or are not *meant* to stay with you. You must make a decision as to whether you leave those people behind. Often, you have to take a detour in order to achieve your goals. Alison Levine, one of a few people to complete the Adventure Grand Slam (this means she has climbed the Seven Summits and skied to both the North and South Poles), talks about how you lose people when you go to each summit.[1] In her TED talks, she shares how she pushed forward by leaving a few unfit people behind. Before reaching summit five, they turned around and climbed down the mountain. The decision

---

[1]Allison Levine, *On the Edge: The Art of High-Impact Leadership*, Grand Central Publishing, Published in 2014, https://www.grandcentralpublishing.com/titles/alison-levine/on-the-edge/9781455544875/

to descend 800 feet from the top of Mount Everest saved her life, even though she failed to reach the Summit, it prepared her to scale the beast 8 years later.

If you lose critical people, or even a co-founder, continue to network. You'll find talented people out there. These people should complement your skill set and carry plenty of knowledge with them. Look at their personality as much as their skill set. A lot of founders I work with, the bright ones, like Marketo founder Phil Fernandez, do not allow politics to get in the way. One time, our sales director and I had a meeting with a Fortune 100 customer. The sales leader would not sync up with me prior to the call. After the meeting, we went to Phil and told him it did not go well. As I typically do, I accepted responsibility. "It was my fault," I said. "I should have canceled and rescheduled knowing I did not have the information I needed."

> "Who owns sales?"
> The sales leader said he did.
> Phil replied, "Then go fix that and come back to me."

Phil was bright. He knew the landscape. His judgment was sharp. In contrast, at another company, I worked for an inexperienced founder who would blame the Customer Success team for the mess sales left behind, which led to a parade of poor judgments and resulted in high turnover. *This* is the difference between an experienced and inexperienced founder.

Onward

Along our adventure, when we got stuck for hours, I thought our trip was going to end quickly in disaster. Losing a day on the mountain is dangerous. You have to drive at night, and you can't see anything in front of you. You could easily fall off the cliff. There were other times when Hassan had to talk to workers, asking them to unblock the road. He was creative, and always found ways to get us unstuck. He would get out of the car and talk with people, sometimes paying them. He always found a way through. I was not sure about him, to be honest, when I first met him. I had questions: "Can he do this? Can he carry us on this journey successfully?"

To this day, I can still see him clearly in my mind. Hassan. The man who got us unstuck, moving forward, making progress on a cold, tall mountain.

Your journey through the Move Product to Market Camp might be edged in doubt at times, but when you're confident about your MVP, product category, and team, you begin to feel momentum—and the reality that scaling your start-up is within reach.

Chapter 4

GO FROM MARKET TO SCALE CAMP

Every step of this journey is messy, hard and seemingly impossible. Adversity climbs with us.

Our camera breaks. The winds pick up, and temperatures plummet. A river rises, a warning sign says STOP. We press on. My mind wanders to odd places. I think of movies famous for using slow motion. Did film director John Woo (*Mission Impossible 2* and *Face/Off*) climb tall mountains and thus get inspired by the slowing of time in his Hong Kong cinematic work? If artists create from what they know, has he experienced my hesitant steps plodding forward as though I'm stepping into a hard wind?

I am flying now—or standing still, I am not sure. The higher I go, the more breaths I take for every step. I am lonely. In the beginning, there were many people on this journey with me. The excitement among all of us was contagious. Now, one by one, they drop.

My early enthusiasm turns to resignation. My climb has evolved. I have evolved. If I look down, the drop is 18,000 feet. How could I come so far but feel like I've barely started? In the daytime, the sun warms the snow, melting it just enough to cause the surface below my boots to shift slightly. Risk nips at our heels. Suddenly, a cloud moves in and blocks everything. Just as quickly, the cloud moves on. In a few minutes, the view is completely different.

I see a sign. It reads: "Beyond this point is for professional climbers only." In my mind, I had thought I would feel elated but, after coming all this way, I feel inadequate. I know this is not the spot I was meant to leave Grandma's ashes. I feel it. She would have wanted me to go further; to show my strength and courage in a larger way. I must go higher. To go as far as all the other tourists went didn't feel grand enough.

I waver: Do I take the risk to cross the river? I cannot see the pole on the other side. I do not know the distance. This is an executive decision. I cross and walk another mile to see. I check the time: 2 p.m. I only have two hours before darkness would fall. At the river's edge, there are 10 people. Besides myself, all but one turn back. Should I follow the group? Doubt creeps in. As the group walks away, so does my comfort level about going forward. If I get stuck or disoriented, I risk my life.

So, I continue. Alone. My Sherpa will go only as far as the sign, because he would lose his job if he does not follow the warning on the sign. Taking an inexperienced climber onward would end his career.

I press on.

My breath plunges into cold air with the same ferocity my boots crush the white, crunchy snow. I plod knee-high through the river. I don't know what is ahead of me, but I know I want a better spot, one that I feel comfortable and at ease with, a spot where my grandmother would feel it is right to lay her ashes.

My breathing is labored, my steps are slow. It takes an hour to walk half a mile at 18,000 feet. The river is up to my knees. I roll up my pants, take off my shoes, and put on a pair of waterproof hiking boots in order to cross. Along my ascent, I wasn't happy about the weight those boots added to my already heavy pack. But now, I am beyond grateful.

Where I am is where most people turn back. The river is freezing cold; it is like walking through a pool of ice just warm enough to be in a liquid state. After crossing the river, I use my towel to wipe down my legs and put my climbing boots back on. I walk another mile. Suddenly, a gray flagpole appears.

Mount Everest Base Camp 18,654 feet.

I immediately know that I can rest Grandma here. During peak time, professional climbers set up camp at this exact spot. But this is the off-season. There is only one other person walking within distance. I do not know her.

I bury the ashes. It is done. I am in the right spot.

Suddenly, my mind is ahead of where I stand. I begin to worry about getting down. The adrenaline that has prodded me forward is nowhere in sight. Darkness is coming fast.

Time is surely not my friend. It is a strange feeling: You know you have achieved a certain level of success, yet you do not embrace the milestone. I am fearful. I do not have my Sherpa. No communication device to call someone. Exhaustion wants to win. If I could just lay down for a moment, but I must descend. A thought seeps in through the fog in my brain: *I already got here. I can't just give up. Giving up would mean failure to the entire mission.*

My teal sweater top, jeans, and scarf look out of place on this mountain. I did not bring the right clothes—with one exception. I have my ski outfit, one of the few luxuries I allowed myself before the trip, and one which I saved for many months. Most climbers wear dri-fit, but I could not afford that. The temperature drop in a given day is like Dr. Jekyll and Mr. Hyde.

My pulse quickens with fear. I do not know how I got here. I feel relieved to keep my promise. It is complicated, so many colliding thoughts. Like a marathoner crossing the finish line, I cannot fully take in this moment. Quick and short.

Then I see a slender young woman. She is from San Francisco. There is no small talk. We just meet, two strangers utterly exhausted, each with a story we do not share. The mountain connects us, and we are happy to see each other. We take pictures of one another.

I regret not having her name or a picture of her. I bet she's another entrepreneur from Silicon Valley (hopefully she'll read this book!). We are the only 2 people out of 200 who made it that day. This, to me, is astonishing because there were so many points I wondered if I would make it.

It is getting dark. We take photos of the most beautiful sunset I've ever seen. Just when the Sherpa and driver are about to call a rescue crew, they see me from a distance. Relief washes over my Sherpa, and he breathes deeply. Later, he says, "You are so lucky, the cloud would always be covering something. Some climbers see sunrise, some see sunset, some don't see anything. The four groups before ours couldn't see anything at all. You have seen it all." He adds, "The mountain is very strange." Had he not told me, I would never have known. I would have thought everything we experienced was universal, normal, everyday. We don't know what we don't know in life.

Secretly, I smile. I know it is Grandma's blessing.

Go From Market To Scale Camp

Typically, in many start-ups, here's the roll call. As soon as you have a real product, you hire a sales leader. Marketing and HR follow. Once those positions are full, you need someone to onboard customers. Then tech support. Then accounting. Then legal counsel.

Do you see the big miss? Oftentimes, founders ignore the channel until it's almost too late. What do you do with these partners? This position should be moved up along with services—especially when you have enterprise partners like Amazon, Microsoft, or Salesforce. Otherwise, it's difficult to gain traction.

In the Go From Market to Scale Camp, you fix the broken link of the Product/Market Fit Disconnect, a critical shortcoming that holds many companies back from thriving later on. Most people don't figure out product/market fit until much later in the game. The reason? Because we don't know what we don't know in life. We just keep going. Marketing momentum, though, will only get you so far.

Product market fit tells you if your product is marketable. This is where a perfectionist mindset comes in handy!

What founders feel at this stage: fear.

Here, you will spend some time shifting your attention between two important areas: distribution channel strategy and scaling your customer.

We begin with channel architecture. When you go to market, validate your market segmentation. Who are the other key players? Channel strategy is a force multiplier to drive additional revenue acceleration. The size of potential outcome that you are driving with enterprise, mid-market, and small business leads to measurable results.

Decision #10: What Distribution Channel Will You Build As a Pathway to Customers?

At this point along your ascent, you know your competitive landscape. You have a fully integrated brand, and you can see some traction—before you go to market. Now it's time to focus on your distribution channel. Early miscalculations often result in products mismatched to market demand. The match must be perfect. "Slightly off" is still off.

Go-to-Market Strategy

Sometimes, people confuse go-to-market strategy with product/market fit. There's a difference. A go-to-market strategy is a step-by-step roadmap to launching your product in a shorter period of time. "A **product-market fit** means being in a good market with a product that can satisfy that market," says start-up coach and investor Marc Andreessen. When you identify a need in the market and build a solution that customers want to buy, that's product-market fit.

Your product-market fit evolves depending on your growth stage, buyer journey attributes, product characteristics, channel capacity, deal structure, verticals, ecosystem, partner dynamic, geographics, and pricing strategy.

Identify market segmentation and shape strategy for distribution channels.

Product Distribution Channels

Channels	Typical Scenario	Market Segmentation	When to Consider
BDRs (cold call reps)	Least marketing effort	*Small Business	High velocity deals with shorter sales cycles
Direct Sales	Lead generated for sales to follow-up	**Mid-market & ***Enterprise	Top priority segment growth can be accelerated via sales reps
Co-Marketer	Two companies commit to promote	Mid-market & Enterprise	Your solution is complementary to your co-marketers
Independent Software Vendors (ISV)	Sell software into specific verticals	Financial Services, Healthcare, etc.	Vertical penetration with domain expertise needed
Original Equipment	OEM owns white label product go-to-market and post-sales support	Manufacturing, Technology, or where there is a fit	Unfamiliar or highly regulated market penetration
Reseller	Pays wholesale price and sells at their own price	Any Market	Gain competitive advantage leveraging reputable resellers
System Integrator (SI)	Optimizes company workflow via integration of your solution	Enterprise, Global footprint, Complex use cases, highly regulated verticals	Enterprise scale-up with consistent customer on-boarding and partner enablement
Online Marketplace	Charge you by transaction (2-35% of selling price)	Salesforce App Exchange, eBay, Amazon, iTunes	Consider how this would impact your financials and support capacity

*Small Business: Employees < 100, Revenue < $50M
**Mid-Market: Employees 100-1000, Revenue $50M to $1B
***Enterprise: Employees >1000, Revenue > $1B

Know the buyer journey and customer engagement model for each sales stage.

Mapping out buyer journeys (top, mid, and bottom funnel) will help you determine which distribution channel is a better fit for you. For example, the typical go-to-market challenge for top funnel is to create brand awareness. Direct sales or BDRs can help, along with lead generation through marketing, while ISVs, SI, and Resellers can accelerate market reach.

Understanding your buyer process is a critical step to come up with a sound go-to-market strategy. The buyer process encompasses sales stages, description of each stage, objective of each stage, stage owner, resources involved, key activities and customer/prospect outcomes, internal sales tools used, external sales and marketing collaterals needed, and customer engagement for each stage.

Use a data-driven approach to ensure financial health and viability.

Successful companies clearly define how they measure success through metrics by segment, product, channel, sales region, marketing program, and customers. There are three leading indicators to track the health of SaaS companies:

1. LTV (lifetime value of customer) refers to gross profit per customer over average customer lifetime. If a customer purchases $10,000 worth of products or services from your business over the lifetime of your relationship, and the total cost of sales and service to the customer is $5000, then the LTV is $5000.

2. CAC (cost of acquiring customer) refers to marketing and sales costs divided by number of customers. For example, if a company spent $1000 on marketing, $2000 on sales in a year, and acquired 200 customers in the same year, their CAC is $15.

3. Payback period on CAC refers to the time it takes for a customer to pay back their customer acquisition costs. For example, A customer that costs $600 in sales and marketing spend to acquire and contributes $500/month, or $6000/year, has a payback period of 1.2 month or 0.1.

What's considered healthy? LTV/CAC > 3; and payback >0.75 are indicators that your company outperforms. Otherwise, you should revisit your product-market fit and go-to-market strategy.

Focusing on unlocking the lifetime value of your customer will result in accelerated growth, as the CAC is much lower on install-based customers than new customers.

Decision #11: What is Your Pricing Strategy?

Many founders start with the costs to make a product when it comes to figuring out price. However, I would encourage you to set all that aside because you want your pricing to be tied to *value*. Who are your targeted buyers? What is their ability to pay? How much pain is your ICP in? Understand the customer acquisition cost (CAC) per dollar of annual contract value (ACV). CAC is much higher for new customer acquisition compared to the upsell, cross-sell, or a renewal on an existing customer. On average, 50 to 70% of revenue growth comes from expansion revenue. Design your pricing and upsell strategy with this in mind. Explore all your competitive alternatives. Pricing vision comes about from the customer's ability to pay and the persona of your buyers.

Timing also comes into play. Are you at the stage of penetrating a new market or expanding into an existing market?

Early-stage start-ups are desperate; they rush to give things away for free. When a customer gets something for free, they may not be serious about your investment. When you have to give something for free, either you don't have a strong value proposition or did not articulate the value well. And sometimes you get to know the customer and learn about them and get engaged, somehow losing focus on converting them into a buying customer. The long game is solving the problem. No contest there. You need to pilot your product. Agreed. However, strategic pricing reflects the value you're bringing to the table.

Supply and demand analysis. What is the degree of pain? What is the economic value of relieving that pain? How is your competitive solution priced?

Price to penetrate the market for SaaS models. If you're offering a freemium, you need to have a practice in place so you understand the conversion criteria for turning that free customer into a paying customer. If they don't convert, figure out why. Maybe it was not the right target. If this is the case, shift your product focus or your ICP.

Two pricing methods we'll explore here are extension pricing and competitive pricing.

Extension pricing. According to the MBA Skool Team, extension pricing is "a strategy where a company has standard prices for its products across all locations and geographies irrespective of any other factors. In such a case, shipping, taxes and other expenses are covered in the standard price. It is one of the pricing strategies used by companies."

Competitive pricing. Investopedia describes competitive pricing as "the process of selecting strategic price points to best take advantage of a product or service-based market relative to competition."

If you have customers in multiple markets, you want to make sure your pricing doesn't backfire. Let's say you have an enterprise client with locations in both China and the United

Kingdom. If you are negotiating on a corporate level, can you afford a discount to a region for large, global customers? Your customers talk to each other, so be mindful. What is the value of that discount, and does the customer really appreciate it? One discount might get you a customer but may not help you scale.

Lastly, pricing needs to be simple. It should get to a point where adding on more products and pricing the platform and add-on features is a piece of cake.

Decision #12: How Will You Help Your Customer's Customer Scale and Grow?

You hear companies tout all the time about how customer-centric they are. But what does that really mean? True customer-centricity focuses not only on your direct customer, but also on your customer's customer. When your customers rely on your solution to scale and grow, you become an essential solution provider and have a much higher chance of creating not just a customer, but a brand evangelist. This is when they expand their footprint with you, and you can accelerate growth through both upselling and cross-selling.

Be intentional about the steps you take to keep the customers of your customer driving success. In other words, make them look good, act bravely, and deliver on your customers' brand promises.

Scaling your customer's customer brings the Minimum Viable Repeatability Disconnect squarely in your line of sight. Test with a customer use case and segmentation. Many call this the product roadmap. It's easy for founders to get caught up in execution by measuring schema. Instead, focus on your product strategy—your value prop for the company and your brand identity. Then, align your product strategy through execution. The product differentiation is so critical. The best way to test your product vision is to partner with a customer. When you're observing your solution in real time, ask:

- Does your product satisfy the market you intend to target?
- Does it apply to multiple verticals or segments?
- Which market segment (B2B vs. B2C; SMB, Mid-Market or Enterprise) or vertical does your product fit the best?
- What are the multiple layers in place to test the product?
- If there are multiple products, do you have an aligned pricing strategy?
- Is your channel distribution strategy aligned with your go-to-market strategy?
- Does your revenue increase without substantial increase of resources or efforts?

Onward

You are a little more than halfway up the start-up mountain. I am proud of you for having the courage and grit to stay the course. On the next leg of your journey, the air will get a little thinner, and you might notice a few surprises—like what you *thought* your customer wanted was really something very different. Or that your product's features were not quite as important as your service responsiveness. Or that what keeps your customer up at night is actually much more relevant to you than the literal solution you provide. The next milestone along your journey is, in fact, one of the most important. It is acclimating to the voice of your customer.

Shortly, you'll be taking a few steps forward—and a few more than that backward. This is how we acclimate to higher altitude. This is also how you dig deep to understand the people you built your solution for in the first place.

Chapter 5

ACCLIMATE TO THE VOICE OF CUSTOMER CAMP

I have not showered for 10 straight days, the longest duration since immigrating to the United States. This is hard for a regimented person like me who could happily wash my hair twice a day.

I shake my head to bring myself back into focus. I am on a tall mountain doing the work I set out to do. The "why" behind my climb is to keep a sacred promise to Grandma. *She would be proud that I came so far,* I think. The thought vanishes. There isn't a moment to lose. I know more climbers are killed on the way down than on the way up. I never thought I could have made it this far. Danger and risk have been constant companions along this journey. The possibility of death, though, has never been more real than at this moment.

I've got to figure out how to get myself down. I must summon the energy to descend. This moment is not as glamorous as novels portray. I have diarrhea, a physical reaction common for climbers enduring high altitudes. My body feels numb. My decision-making is not sharp, so I lean on my Sherpa guide, the people around me, all that I have done to prepare, and the steely grit of my grandmother. There is no choice but to bear the challenge: mental, physical, emotional, spiritual. I am willing to give my life to reach my mission, but I will fight for my life all the same.

I cross a river. I am knee-high in freezing water. At the time, the road was not well-made. It was 2007, the year before the Olympics in China, where torchbearers ran the torch relay in honor of the 2008 Summer Olympics up Mount Everest.[1] Had I waited one more year, the path would have been greatly improved. Today, if a car flips, everyone in it becomes part of the valley. They will never be found. Our experienced Sherpa guides me. My life is now one part luck, one part determination. Our Sherpa reminds me we are the only ones who can see the sunset and sunrise that week at Base Camp. Our eyes feast on majestic white-capped mountains inserted like hundreds of triangles against a backdrop of cerulean blue. The scene before me reminds me of my smallness and my greatness all at once. "Make the world proud," I hear Grandma say.

My grandmother's spirit drives me forward. She makes this happen. I feel relief in having carried her ashes to this tall mountain. I had no doubt I would succeed. Perhaps, though, others felt the same way. Being one of the only ones that day to make it 18,000 feet above sea level, I am reminded that having a goal is not enough. I realize the profound marriage between understanding *why* you are doing something and your success.

---

[1]Wikipedia, 2008 Summer Olympics summit of Mount Everest https://en.wikipedia.org/wiki/2008_Summer_Olympics_summit_of_Mount_Everest

I go back to the cabin with its tiny wooden bed and no mattress. My blanket is like a thin throw you'd use for a sofa. Again, I am grateful for the protection of my blue ski outfit. The bed is hard and cold. Everything I have is the bare minimum for a human being. Sleep does not come easy during the night. Sirens blare. People are taken down the mountain because their bodies could not acclimate to the high altitude.

It has nothing to do with capability or skill. It's luck.

But I know this is not completely true either because our journeys are also marked by a thousand decisions along the way. My mind drifts again, going back and then further back.

Acclimate To The Voice Of Customer Camp

This camp is about "stepping back to move forward." Acclimating to the voice of your customer is where you drive growth and pull away from the pack while differentiating your brand. You are the only one with your story. Here is where you explore your start-up through the lens of your customer, constantly revalidating and aligning your strategy with your execution plan.

Let's first take a look at the basic concept of acclimating, a requirement whether you are scaling Everest or scaling a tech start-up.

Acclimate: to adapt to a new temperature, altitude, climate, environment or situation.[1]

---

[1] Merriam-Webster dictionary, "Acclimate – intransitive verb", https://www.merriam-webster.com/dictionary/acclimate

For founders, acclimating to the voice of customers means solving the Customer Voice Disconnect. Customers will tell you what they want. Sometimes, they'll even tell you what you want to hear. "Everything's fine!" or "We're just considering other options" or "We're making a few changes here, so I'll circle back later." Your ability to listen and dig deeper to understand what their words *really* mean will set you apart from your competition.

Stay close to customers who invested in you and have been offering advice along the way. Leave the "lab" and listen—or have someone who knows what to listen to do the work to understand what your customer feels throughout their journey with you.

Getting the contract signed is only the beginning of your customer journey. Real success comes when you understand why your customer is investing in you in the first place—and what their expectations are along the way—in order to validate their decision, grow with you, and eventually become your greatest advocate.

As companies reach beyond 100 customers, they start feeling overwhelmed and risk losing the intimate relationship with their customers as they find it challenging to scale at the accelerated pace they're used to. The teams end up spending more time on tactical support ticket resolution and renewal discussions rather than proactive outreach to understand what really matters to their customers. To scale, companies should be obsessed with their customer's lifetime value and have a dedicated customer success team focusing on driving customer adoption.[1]

[1] Helen Yu, "Customer Success Obsession: Disruption or Disruptor?" In Motion, Published March 19, 2019 https://www.staterinmotion.com/feed/customer -success-obsession-disruption-or-disruptor?rq=Customer%20Success%20 Obsession

The most dangerous mistake is to focus on hunting for new logos while taking install-based customers for granted. Your best customers are those who are engaged with you, and they may demand more of your attention. They are also well-connected, opinionated, and vocal about their experience—and perhaps have established relationships with your competition as well. Losing one customer like that could have ripple effects, especially when they become your competition's customer reference.

Customer concerns need to be addressed in a timely manner. For example, if your customer is concerned with certain product features and threatens to leave you, listen to them and work with the product team to develop a short-term and long-term solution as quickly as possible. Most importantly, take time to understand the business impact on your customer and take proactive action.

It is imperative to understand the root cause of the issue. You should never take your customers for granted—especially customers who can vouch for you, as they are the ones who can make a significant impact on your growth. Create advocates, not just customers. Advocates invest more in you than others. They stay with you through thick and thin, recommend you to others, and forgive you as long as you are committed to course-correct mistakes. They go out of their way to be your champion and expand the footprint of your solution.

Rapid growth is a blessing, but it also demands that you be realistic about what you can deliver. The greater your solution is, the higher demand you generate, and it is likely you will sacrifice the quality of your work to keep up with the demand. At this point, you need to be honest with your customer—

and yourself. The next new customer you take, you must say, "Here's my realistic bandwidth. I may need a little more time." It's better to turn down the business if your solution is not the right fit than to promise what you can't deliver and create an angry ex-customer.

Gaining trust from your customers will not only earn you their loyalty, but also will accelerate your growth through word of mouth. In the SaaS world, customers leave you when they feel the lack of attention, but even more importantly, they will leave you when they experience a lack of honesty. I don't mean to scare you, but when it comes to technology, your product is dispensable and replaceable. Losing one influential customer may have a domino effect—others will eventually follow suit. Customer loyalty is earned through consistent and holistic strategies and is much like a team sport. A customer can leave at any time for a better offering, unless you make them believe that they can't build a future without your thought leadership and guidance.

Every customer is different. Understanding the uniqueness of that customer becomes priority one. Ask: What does success look like to your customer? How do they measure that success? Is that aligned with your understanding? These insights will help you prioritize your engagement and focus on what matters to your customer.

What founders feel at this stage: a sense of wonder and confidence.

Sometimes, you have to determine if you want to accommodate their requests or turn down the business. For example, if you want to do business with Google, if that is aligned with your long-term strategy, you need to see if you are willing to shift your solution to host it on Google Cloud. If you have already invested heavily on AWS, it may not be the best timing to switch course. What are the requirements for that customer? You have to be open and honest with them. This sounds like common sense, but I've seen a lack of openness and honesty take good companies down. They tried so hard to be "big and corporate" that they forgot to be human.

Decision #13: Is Your Company as Customer-Centric as Your Marketing Content Says It Is?

Every brand wants to be customer-centric. Many emblazon it across their office walls or put it as a differentiator on their about page. The problem is, you can't be customer-centric without a tactical understanding of your customers and an understanding of the Customer Voice Disconnect.

Buzzwords are left for people who don't know how to get to the top. You're different. As a founder, you've got your customer's back for all the right reasons. Go beyond being a solution provider. Set aside survey results. Instead, create a customer experience that drives growth for both your start-up *and* your customer.

Here are the five competencies you should build to become a customer-centric organization:

1. **Treat customers as assets.** Just like your inventory, real estate, and talent are valuable assets, so is your

customer base. Define your performance metric here, whether it's a gain or loss, and understand what drives gains or triggers losses. Connect customer asset management with business impact.

2. **Align intentionally around customer experience.** Be intentional about driving accountability around customer experience. Unforgettable customer experience doesn't happen through luck or chance.

3. **Build an active customer listening path.** Our life stories change over time, and so do the stories of our customers. Listen closely and reimagine the story of the customer journey.

4. **Deliver consistent and reliable customer experience.** Don't wait for your customers to tell you where your CX is faulty. Deliver consistent experiences across the entire customer journey. What are the key customer touchpoints? What are your customers' pivotal moments? When do they need you the most? How do you show up?

5. **Create a culture of accountability around customer experience.** Customer experience is everyone's responsibility. Make NPS or CSAT a common metric to drive accountability around customer experience.

Decision #14: How Will You Get to Know Your Customer?

Let's start broadly. First off, existing and new customers have two different customer journeys. For example, new customers might begin their customer journey with onboarding.

An existing customer doesn't need to be onboarded. They are already going through different stages of their journey with you. With that said, give just as much attention to your existing customer as you give to new ones. While you may not need an onboarding session with them, a quarterly business review is a great way to reconnect, give you an opportunity to better understand their business, and align your priorities with their success going forward. The generally accepted number I have heard is that a new customer costs five times more to acquire than up-selling and cross-selling to an existing customer, so a mix of both will feed your strategy to scale.

Mapping out customer journeys based on each stage of your customer is a process that allows you to better understand your customer's expectations, how you interact with your customer, where the gaps are for process, and key outcome perspectives. It helps you align customer-centric strategy to execution and deliver consistent, reliable customer experience.

Here is a sample customer journey framework:

Customer Journey Framework

Customer Journey Stage	Value Discovery		Value Realization		Value Optimization	
	Evaluate	Invest	Deploy	Adopt	Expand	Advocate
Customer Expectation	Findable	Trustworthy	Speed	Time to Value	Roadmap	Value Prop.
	Stable	Responsive	Success	Alignable	Justification	Case Study
	Solution Fit	Affordable	Risk Management	Change Management	Scale	Advocate
Your Function						
Marketing	A	I	I	I	I	A
Sales	R	A	I	I	A	I
Pre-sales	C	R	I	I	R	I
Services/Partner	C	C	A	C	C	I
Customer Success		C	I	A	R	R
Education		I	R	R	R	I
Support			I	R	R	I
Product	I	I	I	I	I	I
Engineering			I	I	I	I
Operations		R	I	I	I	I

A = Accountable; R = Responsible; I = Informed; C = Consulted

When it comes to customer journey mapping, customers typically go through six stages: **Evaluate, Invest, Deploy, Adopt, Expand, and Advocate.**

Evaluation

You should be an easy-to-find solution your customer is searching for. They Google their problem, and they find you. You need to know what they are looking for: a financially stable company, someone who can have shared value with them, and thought leadership. Marketing plays a critical role along with Sales in creating awareness during the evaluation phase.

Investment

There are three things to know in order to drive value-based engagement to secure investment in your solution:

- What is the business outcome your customers are driving? Make sure you focus on what matters to your customer.
- Now, to drive that business outcome, what are the required capabilities they must have? Demonstrate that your solution has all the required capabilities.
- Lastly, how do they measure success? Understand the success criteria helps you better articulate your value proposition.

Show them how your solution solves their problem, how you do it better and differently than your competition, and where else you have successfully delivered a similar solution with demonstrated success.

Deployment

As a new customer goes through an onboarding process to deploy your solution, they expect your service team has experts who can guide them through the design and implementation process. Your service team can leverage the opportunity to build trust with customers and drive deployment success. Don't forget to celebrate each milestone of the deployment. Recognizing team members and customers for their contribution to the deployment success makes it a rewarding journey for all.

Adoption

Your customer success team is responsible for driving adoption once your service team completes customer onboarding. Low adoption is an indicator that the solution is not fully bought-in and prone to customer churn risk. This is why it is critical to invest in customer success to understand the key drivers that accelerate adoption for your solution. Most importantly, keep track of your customer adoption. Make them stick around. Removing barriers to their adoption will reduce the risk of losing customers.

Expansion

After experiencing some success, your customers are expanding their footprint with you. What is the customer use case that triggered the expansion? Is it repeatable for other customers? Keep your sales team in the loop as you see opportunities to expand the footprint. Your customer success team should partner with the sales team to convert these up-sell and cross-sell opportunities.

Advocacy

Turning your customer into a reference is what you strive for. This is where your customer success team collaborates with marketing to turn happy customers into success stories. Remember to build multiple layers of advocacy for the same customer to avoid loss triggered by stakeholder changes.

Next, don't go too high or too fast up the mountain. Acclimate to the voice of your customer thoughtfully. One of the most effective ways of acclimating to the voice of customers is to build customer rooms. This means that if you hear any feedback on a feature request, you take it to the head of engineering to help influence the product roadmap, you reach out to customers at each important key moment to collect feedback, and you share it with internal stakeholders. Key moments might include: project kickoff, customer go-live, customer sponsor departure, customer renewal, customer M&A, your executive departure, or your resource turnover.

Build the Customer Room

Welcome to the customer room, where you are the lucky start-up that gets to know your customer's deepest expectations. Building customer rooms is an exercise that aligns cross-functional teams around customer experience and holds them accountable.

Customer Room

Onboarding	Adoption	Expansion	Advocacy
Implementation Stage	Adoption Maturity	Opportunity to Up-Sell	Customer References
Plan	Crawl*	ARR by Product	ICP Verticals
Build	Walk*	Services	Competitive Wins
Test	Run*	Premium Support	Partner Success
Deploy	Grow*	Education	Use Cases by Product
Support		Multi-Year	Success by Regions
Ensure Successful Onboarding	**Improve Customer LTV**	**Footprint Expansion**	**Drive Brand Advocacy**

* The definition of crawl, walk, run, and grow determines your customer's adoption maturity

The **Onboarding room** is owned by the professional service team. With effective management, you can tell how many customers are going through the onboarding process in a given time period, which drives hiring or partnering decisions.

The **Adoption room** is owned by the customer success team. This is where you put your customer under three buckets: crawl, walk, run to measure their adoption maturity. The definition can be unique depending on your business. Figuring out how you can increase customer adoption maturity will get you on the path of scaling.

The **Expansion room** is owned by Sales. This is where you identify each customer with upsell and cross-sell opportunities, including other products/solutions or services.

The **Advocacy room** is owned by marketing. This is where your referenceable customers reside. This advocacy room helps you understand the use case, vertical and product line, and geographic location of your references. This is where your customer success team collaborates with the marketing team to create customer success collateral.

Acclimating to the voice of your customer requires a strategic mindset. This means not taking anything for granted and not making assumptions. Focus on the value exchange conversation with your customer. For example, one of my customers was just acquired by a private equity company that I worked with. I reached out to their CEO and offered some insights on what to anticipate.

What does success look like for your customer? What success looked like a year ago may not look like success today.

Leadership changes. You must understand the value exchange. Value means different things to different people: A CMO equates value with brand awareness and lead generation. A CEO might look at overall company growth. A CIO regards value according to their cybersecurity track record.

Understand your customer's problem—the value drivers for each stakeholder and solving their problem is how you expand the lifetime value of your customers and unlock the growth potentials. This is where you look for the Minimal Viable Repeatability (MVR) for your go-to-market and customer experience. Figure out the rhythm of what makes your customers successful. What triggers their success and drives responsible growth? How do you repeat that success?

For example, when I joined Marketo, the service team didn't get involved until the Enterprise deal was closed. We ran into the challenge of sales over-promising and service under-delivering due to the Process Disconnect. So, I asked the question, "Why do we do it this way?" The response was that our services did not have savvy resources to support sales.

I met with 10 Enterprise customers consisting of CIOs and CMOs. I asked them all the same question: "What does success look like to you?" Most CMOs said that, simply put, they are not challenged by technology. They struggled with marketing automation in general. The marketing landscape was wide. Most companies have CRM, demand generation tools, content marketing, email marketing, search engine optimization, social media marketing, advertising, and website analytics. Their website consisted of 10 to 15 different platforms (that's way too many!). They wanted to better understand how they were doing compared to competitors and where to start.

What should customers do prior to adopting a marketing automation solution? What impact on organizational competency and enablement should they anticipate post-adoption of the solution? That was what mattered. So, we ventured to build a marketing automation adoption roadmap based on their maturity and helped them scale by solving their problem through each stage of their journey with us. We took them through the entire business process and took the "struggle" away—from assessment to end goal.

With that, we created a digital marketing practice, getting CMOs' buy-in during the sales cycle in larger enterprise deals and helping them build a marketing automation blueprint during the onboarding process.

When I talked to CIOs, they said marketing automation had a small footprint. They wanted to better understand how marketing automation fit into their overall architecture and impact on security, user experience, infrastructure, and data flow. What implications does it have on IT for a global deployment? What requests belong to IT vs. business? What is the data flow? Do companies move data from marketing automation to another system or bi-directional?

From these conversations, I realized that we needed team members with technical expertise beyond Marketo. For example, we needed people who were experts in Salesforce, Adobe, and Microsoft Dynamic. We launched an Integration Practice.

The intent of creating the Digital Marketing and Integration practices was not to increase service revenue, but rather increase our interaction with CMO/CIO/CTOs. And guess what? Our efforts expanded license deals and earned us our first million-dollar service deal (the gong was struck, and champagne was poured!).

Both CMOs and CIOs were concerned about the lack of knowledge around marketing automation. They could not come up with concrete recommendations. I learned that they attempted to develop an internal training curriculum without success. Their lack of knowledge for marketing automation was holding them back (and keeping us from getting the deal). So, we expanded our education offering to include "User Passport." This named user training offering is renewable and allows users to pick and choose up to a certain number of trainings based on their personal needs. The pricing increases for each of the five incremental types of training the user chooses. We then added a certification program for partners and customers. People felt accomplished, confident, and viewed Marketo as a trusted partner.

That's part of the story behind Marketo scaling to become a top-rated marketing automation contender.

Culture of Accountability Around the Customer Experience

Paris and Chicago were 50 degrees and rainy the day I heard back from my toughest client, the head of a large French multinational corporation. His email made me realize he and

I had more in common than I ever thought possible—much more than just the weather.

A few weeks previously, he had given us an unbelievably hard time: questioning our value, asking for extra services, being brutally abrupt. His words on that balmy day, however, were 180 degrees different.

He wrote that my team was "in his heart during this time of extraordinary difficulties, because when you choose a partner, it is not just to move forward during those times when the sun is shining—it is also to be on the same side when adversity and challenges are coming."

It wasn't the praise; it was the truth that touched me. Somehow, through all the difficult conversations, our companies had become true partners.

I believe remarkable customer experiences happen when people rise above the expected. You set aside what is important to you when you wake up that particular morning and, instead, really listen to the other person. Partnerships grow when you show you are committed. This is the long game that many companies miss.

CX expectations are higher than what short-term perspective can satisfy. You have to stay three, five, and ten months ahead.

Delivering remarkable CX means protecting our customers when they least expect it. What does this paradigm look like?

Customers are loyal. They talk about their experience with others. They feel understood, valued, and heard. They feel joy working with you, choosing you, buying your products, experiencing your services, and investing their time with you. There's an emotional connection. They trust you.

For me, exploration begins with curiosity. Here are seven steps to explore to elevate the customer experience.

1. Existing Customers and a Customer Impact Analysis

During the pandemic, I had customers who were severely impacted. The last thing they wanted to do was to talk to a vendor. Other customers were growing. This is where we had to tailor our engagement with customers based on their needs. And so do you.

Here's how I went about this. At the start of the pandemic, I did a customer impact analysis, categorized them, and then developed an outreach plan for each. We tailor actions and communication to customer needs after a deep portfolio review. What are their challenges in the new normal? Is their priority the same or different from two months ago? What matters to them most?

It's tedious to refocus because every customer is different. Remapping customer journeys does not solve the issue. There's no immediate Rx to fix this. It takes work. I spoke to one customer who lost someone to the virus. There was nothing I could say or do except to give them my heartfelt grief and let them know we were there for them.

2. Guiding Customers through the Buying Process

The buying process and investment decisions change with external influences. How do you navigate customers through sudden, drastic change? Lean on your customer journey framework—and then guide them.

Take the stress out of the buying process. Help them be more effective with a digital selling perspective. Show that you support them. Success comes by way of how we show up in trying times, and is where we find sustainable growth and build trust. How can they maximize operational efficiency? How do you manage a remote workforce to drive CX? How do you deliver remarkable CX consistently?

Take this time to differentiate your brand and capitalize on the success you already have achieved. Drive the experience that matters most to your customer.

3. Your Communication Protocol is Awesome, Right?

RIGHT? Hellooooo? Are you still there? OK, seriously, communication is a must-have in any great relationship. It is two-way; a dialogue where each person feels valued and heard.

Now, with that said, we've all had instances where we promised to follow up with a customer, and then, oops! It fell through the cracks. This happens more often, however, when you don't have a protocol in place.

Focus on internal customers first—your team. Blossom this out to external customers. Then, over-communicate. Change the workflow if you have to, but strive to improve the communication process at every customer touchpoint. If you don't have a communication protocol, build it now.

Really listen to what customers have to say. Listening technology, social media monitoring, surveys, monitoring customer reviews, and market segmentation are ways to understand the voice of your customer. Nothing, however, beats an actual conversation with a strong CX leadership.

Build customer confidence through content that uses their language. Share notes from customer conversations across your sales and marketing team. Learn from each other. Enable one another to deliver a great customer experience.

4. The People Responsible for Remarkable CX

Most would agree that customer success starts with our understanding of the customer. So, whose job is this? The obvious answer is the customer success team. But, pinning CX on one department is a limited worldview.

The customer sees far more than what we show them. They see our values in one-on-one conversations. They learn about our mission through the causes we support. They experience our brand in the decisions our board of directors make.

Here's a look at CX from various levels of an organization.

The board: Many brands talk about being customer-centric. Yet, 70% of company boards do not have people with CX experience, according to a report from Dimension Data. The report says this is "where companies talk about CX, but fail to deliver on it." Why? It is much harder to adapt to the voice of your customer when that voice is not recognized during the strategic planning process.

The CEO: A great CEO proactively manages communication operations with direct reports every day and communicates with the entire team. He reaches out to investors on industry trends. He makes sure team members and their families are healthy. You cannot expect anything better than proactive communications.

Another step for a leader to take is getting prepared for the future of work. How do you adapt to a changing reality? How do you prepare and manage a remote workforce? If that day comes, and it will come at scale, how will you be prepared?

The executive team: Lead by example. If there is a hit, the leaders must take the hit first. Servant leadership has never been more important. We should not expect our teams to do things without our leaders doing them first.

The frontlines: Focus on quality interactions. Give customer-facing team members a deep understanding of the customer. Show them how to inspire confidence and understand customer challenges with tailored messages and approaches.

As you've probably figured out, the responsibility for remarkable CX comes down to one simple word: everyone.

5. Know What You're Willing to Give—Before You Negotiate

You really want the customer renewal. I mean, REALLY want to ink the deal. Financial concessions may seem like a faster way to close, but sometimes it backfires. Discounting is expected in times of crisis and raging market fluctuations. Many companies surviving the Great Recession did so because they yielded to customers' financial situations.

However, you must be strategic about discounting so that it doesn't become learned behavior or mistaken as a lack of confidence in your product. Pricing is a market positioning issue. How you handle pricing is an extension of your brand. Consider your approval process, a discount guideline, and financing options.

With millions of jobs lost in 2020 due to the pandemic, the principal takeaway is understanding the industry of your customer. What can you do to help them endure and thrive?

6. Measuring Remarkable CX

According to the Temkin Group, companies that earn $1 billion annually can expect to earn, on average, an additional $700 million within three years of investing in customer experience. SaaS companies can expect to increase revenue by $1 billion.

These figures come from micro-engagements that lead to customers feeling and realizing success. What defines success for your customers? How will you impact those factors? When this happens, how will you measure success?

7. Be Their Greatest Defender

We are remembered most by how we have served our customers. While we all feel a sense of uncertainty sometimes, one thing remains unchanged. When customers know your company is there for them, they become hopeful and uplifted. You will be the one to protect them over time, through good and bad.

You will be the one to help them thrive.

Decision #15: Are You Willing to Step Back In Order to Move Forward and Acclimate to the Voice of Your Customer?

Sometimes, you must step back in order to move forward. That's where you recharge yourself, reconnect with others, learn from your failures, and find what worked in your start-up's successes. In fact, stepping backward is how you acclimate. On Everest, climbers go from Base Camp to Camp 1 and back to Base Camp. They then go from Base Camp to Camp 2 and back to Base Camp. They then do this a third time to Camp 3. Each time, they learn and add to their arsenal of knowledge, modify their strategy, and adjust things that were not working.

As the founder or CEO, the more you step away from the day-to-day, the bigger chance of success you will have. You can see the forest, learn more about what's happening in the industry to enrich your experience, and learn from others while growing personally. You are brilliant. But you don't know what you don't know. If I were to go back to the mountain, I would pack differently and create a different experience. I've taken note of what I would do differently, not that I'm planning on another ascent any time soon!

One of the biggest obstacles to reaching your summit is not pausing, listening, learning, or reflecting.

Tesla founder Elon Musk ran out of books to read in his library.[1] Financier Warren Buffet spends five to six hours a day reading.[2] Facebook CEO Mark Zuckerberg strives to read one book every two weeks.[3] Nike CEO Donahoe schedules a "thinking day" about every three months as "pre-scheduled, uninterrupted times to step away from the chaos, zero-base my time, and refocus on the issues that are most important."[4]

Here's the thing: It's not good enough to go backward and learn nothing. The key is to acclimate in different ways, with your customer's feedback being the most significant indicator.

At Marketo, they were successfully growing, went IPO at $60 million, then they needed to pivot to further grow through the Enterprise up-market. This was when I joined. We had to figure out a new go-to-market motion, a new way of servicing customers. We had to revisit our product pricing

[1]Avani Bagga, "Personified: 9 things to know about Elon Musk," The Times of India, Published November 3, 2020, https://timesofindia.indiatimes.com /personified-9-things-to-know-about-elon-musk/photostory/52946986.cms#:~: text=Elon%20Musk%20is%20said%20to,he%20started%20reading%20 Encyclopedia%20Britannica.

[2]Michael Simmons, "Bill Gates, Warren Buffett, and Oprah all use the 5-hour rule. Here's how this powerful habit works," Medium, Published February 25, 2020, https://www.businessinsider.com/bill-gates-warren-buffet-and-oprah-all -use-the-5-hour-rule-2017-7#1-read-1

[3]Trey Williams, "Mark Zuckerberg resolves to read a book every other week in 2015", MarketWatch, Published Jan 5, 2015, https://www.marketwatch.com/story/mark -zuckerberg-resolves-to-read-a-book-every-other-week-in-2015-2015-01-05

[4]Andrey Sergeyev, "Why Leaders Must Have "Thinking Time" in Their Schedule," Timewiser.com, https://timewiser.com/blog/leaders-thinking-time-effectiveness/

and re-prioritize our product roadmap. Our investment paid major dividends.

While adapting means shifting direction at times, acclimating means pausing or restarting to adjust to the "thin air" of demanding markets or those with shrinking margins of error.

Acclimating almost always demands getting out of the weeds and working ON the business strategy, aligning it with execution—not while you are IN the business. A founder's "to-do" list quickly turns into "today's" list. Step away from the linear list of tasks and remind yourself about where you want to take the company. A to-do list gets you focused on the day-to-day, where it's easy to forget the relevancy of articulating your vision. Translate vision into a clear strategy about what to do and not to do. This is an art.

What happens when you skip this step and don't go back to Base Camp?

You lose precious ground. You put your team's efforts in peril. You go to the next level without recharging, and you disappear. When you climb Mt. Everest, you have to get your body acclimated to high altitude. If the helicopter drops you directly to the Summit, you could die. Your ascent began when you started your company, when you first thought of it, because even that one little thought had enough energy to propel you forward, to tap you on the shoulder again and again, vying for your attention.

There is no guarantee you will make it to the top. The peak you want to reach may even change in days marked by constant struggle.

Base Camp is a profound marker that reminds us that sometimes in order to move forward, we have to take a step back.

Decision #16: At the End of the Day, How Will You Define Your Customer Experience?

When it comes to the customer experience, what does the peak look like?

It's a beautiful view. Customers are loyal. They talk about the experience they had with your brand to friends and colleagues. They feel understood. They feel joy working with you, choosing you, buying your products, and experiencing your services. There's an emotional connection. They share your brand on social media. They see content that uses words and phrases THEY use. You are it—they're willing to pay more for your products and services because they trust you. They are a customer for life, and you get the highest honor of all—the honor of giving your customer a lifetime of commitment. Imagine a world where acclimating to the voice of customers becomes your number one differentiator and your number one driver for topline growth.

Customer experience is your leading indicator for success. Every company *talks* about this, but few understand how to approach it. You'll find the word "customer-centric" or, "We're obsessed with our customers" without any evidence to back up these lofty claims. Yet, customers are so important for everyone in the company to truly understand. Be a thought leader in whatever solution you offer. It's not good enough to explore or even define your customer experience; you need to own it.

Marketo co-founder Jon Miller would write in-depth thought leadership pieces on marketing automation. When people think of the definitive guide for marketing, they think of Marketo. People do business with you when they are inspired by your thought leadership and when they see shared value. Every high-quality customer interaction enables growth.

As a Group VP running global services at Marketo, I led the team to redefine expectations for each different role. We rewrote the job description of every single role based on the feedback received from customers. We then created a skill set matrix to map the 100+ team skills with the expectation to figure out where we had gaps serving our customers. That allowed us to make data-driven decisions on when to leverage partners vs. internal team members. It also generates a skill set roadmap to upskill the team.

When you get the customer feedback on a product, you take it to the head of the product to help prioritize the product roadmap. You celebrate the customer going live with the sales team, and help them understand the use cases for success and how to repeat it at other accounts. The CX team should ask customers if they are willing to be your reference post-go-live. They connect the marketing team with referenceable customers. That's how you turn happiness into reusable assets. This is how you build an active customer listening path through a culture of collaboration. This is how you create minimum viable repeatability.

Nuances are in the details. You must understand your customer in-depth. Bear in mind that customer churn is a lagging indicator. The root cause of customer churn could be lack of confidence in your product, services, and support, concerns with your pricing, high resource turnover, inconsistent customer experience, financial stability, or your lack of in-region interaction. Frequent change of CX leaders and structures leads to higher customer churn and hinders company growth.

Many companies do NPS (Net Promoter Score, a scoring system by which customers rate how likely they are to recommend a supplier/vendor). What sets you apart is what you do about your NPS score. In many companies, there are different surveys for different internal teams, but they don't always do cross-functional analysis. That's a disconnect of communication. Do a survey, share the result with cross-functional leaders, and take action on it. Customer success teams should drive changes accordingly. Customers could be happy about the product, but not about service or support.

In my 20 years of customer-facing roles for a few rapidly growing SaaS companies, I learned more about the value of the customer experience than at any other time. Do you know who taught me? It was not our product team or our service team. It was our *customers*. Every time customers opened up their organizations, they trusted us to support their move toward greater success. What we did was profound. We looked out for them and earned their loyalty, making a difference for them with our services and our technology solutions.

Onward

My grandmother taught me the value of thinking independently. I wanted to pursue my passions, not pursue other people's passions.

You, as a founder, are going to find success when you do what you love to do and your solution solves the real problem for customers. Don't be afraid to take a step back to move forward. Remember why you are on this journey and the people you built this solution for. When you feel things are out of balance, lean into that and figure out why. It could mean the difference between achievement and discord.

As you scale the start-up mountain, traveling from Acclimate to the Voice of Customer Camp to the Align Strategy to Process and Execution Camp, you will marvel at a quality growing steadily inside you: confidence. You begin to make decisions with your "why" well-defined, your ideas morphed into a tested product with your customer at the center.

Next up, you'll explore the beauty and wonder of process and measurement. This is where you see your hard work really take off, moving you forward faster and more fearlessly up the start-up mountain.

Chapter 6

ALIGN STRATEGY WITH PROCESS AND MEASUREMENT CAMP

When we first started planning for our Mount Everest expedition, I imagined popping champagne as a way to celebrate its finality. Instead, I am hooked up to an IV. My head is barely attached to my body. Even though my physical state is a wreck, I am changed forever. A clear milestone has been reached, leaving me a different person than when I started the journey.

I reunite with friends who did not finish the climb. They waited for me. They celebrate with me, even though they had to drop halfway through the journey. Amazing.

Even though I did not know Hassan prior to this trip, I had to trust and listen to him. I survived by following his advice. Four dropped out because they didn't listen to him. I was forced to become independent at a very young age in a male-dominated culture. If I was going to make it, I needed to architect the outcome. I knew the choices I made were stepping stones to what I wanted to achieve in life, and, while I didn't have money or guidance, I knew one thing for sure: I didn't want my kids to live the same harsh life I did growing up.

When I chose to leave a prestigious middle school to attend a more mainstream school where there were more opportunities to demonstrate my leadership, I dared to make these decisions for myself. I rebelled against the chorus of voices around me. In a more diverse environment, I found the motivation and drive to help others. The pull to be a "multiplier" began early.

Our past feeds our future.

What is the measure of our success? When faced with two different opinions, who will you listen to? Make room for your inner voice, distinguish between outside noise and wise advice. Then, own your decisions.

For me, on this cold mountain, with a needle in my arm instead of champagne in my mouth, the people I care about around me, and a hot shower somewhere in my near future, there are two metrics.

My climb is over. My promise is fulfilled.

Align Strategy with Process and Measurement Camp

It's all about "the process," says Philadelphia 76ers center Joel Embiid. What's true for a layup is true for a start-up. Success is systemized by establishing processes to make results repeatable and dependable. In the Align Strategy with Process and Measurement Camp, you will gauge how high you plan to ascend with specific business goals along the way, with clear processes to achieve your goals and the success criteria to measure them.

Accountability and alignment are the two traits setting top-performing companies apart from the rest. Most of the companies understand the importance of aligning strategy with execution. Many are challenged to operationalize their vision due to a lack of repeatable process, misaligned priorities, and lack of measurement to drive accountability. Accountability sometimes gets a bad rap. The word immediately makes you think of rules shouted out from the top of the mountain set forth for everyone else to abide by. This is just not true. Real accountability is an awesome opportunity to take ownership of ideas and endeavors. Scaling the start-up mountain is a lot easier if you are not dragging yourself or others up it.

Just like my climb up Mount Everest, the goal of my trip was to keep a sacred promise to Grandma. The criteria for success was to accomplish it safely to make her proud. I would not have made it to the Base Camp if I was not over-prepared with a roadmap, process, and tools planned out ahead of the trip. For example, each of us carried a small container of Grandma's ashes. In the event that we lost one of us, one of the others would pick that container up and carry on with the trip. I had to adapt to changes as I lost each of the four other partners along the way. I listened to my Sherpa and guide when I did not know what to do. I held them accountable for what they were supposed to deliver, and that's my advice when you run into obstacles.

This is the stage where the Process Disconnect can impede growth for start-ups because time is money, and efficiency creates time. Discipline becomes paramount. Let's face it; it's easy to watch minutes and then hours disappear, especially for founders who love to create.

This stage is where you need to take a step back and revisit your strategy. Is it still relevant to where you are? Map your updated strategy to each function. You probably have 100+ employees now. You may have many customers depending on your business. You have an engineering and product team, sales team, marketing team (including demand generation), PR, events, finance team, legal team, customer success team to take care of customer adoption and retention, your consulting team to onboard customers, your support team to handle technical cases, and an operations team to track/monitor performance and HR team for talent acquisition.

Misalignment of priorities will occur unless you set up a few common metrics that drive cross-functional accountability. Setting up OKRs (Objectives and Key Results) at the company level is an effective way to conquer process and measurement disconnect. For example, if Driving Customer Satisfaction ("CSAT" above 95%) is one of your OKRs at the company level, you can then have each department come up with department-specific OKRs to achieve that goal. Your HR team would be measured by talent retention rate while the customer success team would be measured by customer retention rate, and engineering team would be measured by how quickly a product defect is resolved. Sales team would focus more on selling to the right customers where your solution can be deployed successfully. Align each of the

What founders feel at this stage: Thrilled to see the summit, exhausted, lonely.

functions of business with a common OKR, aligning with your overall strategy and defining processes and measurements on how they contribute to your success.

Decision #17: How Will You Apply Your Strengths to Your Weaknesses to Find Your Superpower?

Think about your core business strength. Is it a product? Sales? Vision? Thought leadership? Brand? Service? You can't be renowned for everything, but you *can* be in the lead position for *something*.

Let's look at companies everyone knows. Disney is about the customer experience. Apple is about the product experience. Amazon is about distribution channels. At Adobe, when I joined, we were pivoting to become a digital marketing leader. At the time, digital marketing was a new concept up for interpretation. We sold our vision to Fortune 500 companies and co-developed product features to accelerate the launch of critical capabilities. The customer success team played an integral role in translating customers' requirements into marketable product features. We went through the process of mapping out requirements to product features with associated business impacts. The business impact helped us prioritize these feature requests. We then leveraged our customer service team to gain deep customer insights and took customer vision back to the engineering team in order to lead with our greatest strengths.

That was the time when Adobe just pivoted to Digital Marketing arena. The concept of Digital Marketing was new.

There's a big gap between product design and user expectation. On the flip side, I've seen miles between internal perception and customer perception. That's expected.

Really, it all comes back to creating the ultimate customer experience. This is the end goal. There is no one-size-fits-all. Use your superpower to tackle the customer experience. Many start-ups fail because their biggest strength is only half-baked, or they switch strategies or teams too often before they even give it a test run. The frequent change of leadership team is an indication of inexperienced founders or CEOs. Who do you compare your company to? Who else is on the shortlist with you?

It's time to pick up the sword, summon your superpower, and wield your strength. Can you see the Summit? Setting your start-up apart with your core strength gives you an unencumbered view.

Think strength over weakness. Once you have a strategy in place, apply your strengths to the weakness of a given situation. Break it down. Figure out what you want to really accomplish and how you are going to get there using your superpowers—the one thing your start-up is REALLY good at, like:

- **PRODUCT**. Measure by size of product, features, distribution, and speed of product development. Think Google search engine.

- **SALES**. Measure by sales target. Think Salesforce. Instead of popping the traditional champagne when the well-known enterprise software company reached $10 billion in 2017, CEO Marc Benioff set yet another sales goal: $20 billion.[1] He wasted no time, and guess what? The company reached it. While there's much more that goes into reaching a goal than merely setting it, Salesforce recognizes the power of its sales prowess.

- **ENGINEERING**. Measure by driving agenda and priorities like cloud migration or IoT. Think Oracle—fierce competitive spirit, data-driven, use of product scorecards and how it impacts the broader customer experience, and they invest on the engineering side. During my 4 years at Oracle, they acquired 83 companies. Their engineering team could acquire a company and fully integrate within months. Everything is rolled out efficiently across the company.

- **VERTICAL BUSINESS OPERATION**. Measure by particular competency to an industry or function. If you focus on financial services or health care, then you need to understand regulations associated with these verticals. You will need to branch out to partners with domain expertise if you don't have it internally.

- **BRAND**. You define the tenor and tone of relationship with customers with a consistent brand experience. Translate brand promise into how the company conducts itself.

- **CUSTOMER**. Your decision starts with what will deliver the most to customers. High-performing com-

[1]Ron Miller, "How Salesforce Beat its Own Target to Reach 20B Run Rate Ahead of Schedule," Tech Crunch, Published August 27, 2020, https://techcrunch.com/2020/08/27/how-salesforce-beat-its-own-target-to-reach-20b-run-rate-ahead-of-schedule/

panies unite leaders around the customer experience. Hold people accountable to that in every function of the company. USAA insurance adapts to customer needs, has virtual agents available 24 hours a day, and an accessibility center for assistive technologies.[1]

- **VISION**. Think Amazon. It started as a bookstore and quickly became so much more. Obviously, Amazon needs no introduction for its visionary leadership and customer-centric reputation. The two, in fact, go hand in hand. Those companies touting vision as a strength don't just predict the future, but rather the future buying habits and desires of customers. In the book *Built to Last: Successful Habits of Visionary Companies*, authors Jim Collins and Jerry I. Porras describe visionary companies as being a top institution in a particular industry, being a thought leader, and making a footprint in the world.[2] While companies featured in the book hail from 1950 or before, you don't need to be decades old for vision to be your strength.

- **SERVICE**. Apple is perhaps the most well-known example of service as a strength. I have a friend who has the main Apple phone number on her phone. The min-

---

[1] Elafris, 'When you are having a text-based conversation with an AI agent, you often don't know you are interacting with tech and not a live human being", Elafris.com, Published December 6, 2016, https://www.elafris.com/blog-post /youre-text-based-conversation-ai-agent-often-dont-know-youre-interacting-tech-not-live-human/

[2] Collins, Jim and Porras, Jerry I., *Built to Last: Successful habits of Visionary Companies*, HarperCollins, 1994/1997/2002, p. 2 Published November 2, 2004, https://www.harpercollins.com/products/built-to-last-jim-collinsjerry-i-porras ?variant=32117226274850

ute Katherine has a question or issue with her MacBook Pro, she dials up Apple Support, breezes through a brief series of automated questions, and is connected to a live person. She told me once that she will always be an Apple user for their service alone, no matter the price point or product benefits compared to competitive products. Clearly, customers like Katherine directly impact a company's customer lifetime value (CLV).

- **THOUGHT LEADERSHIP**. Build the brand, and then turn your brand into a platform. One of the Marketo co-founders, John Miller, was well known for his thought leadership in marketing. He was the inventor of the definitive guide for marketers. Jon's thought leadership contributed to Marketo's sustainable growth. As a company, building a product people want to use is just the beginning, because customers buy much more than just your product alone. Building thought leadership is way more challenging and makes the barrier to entry higher. You want to stay competitive and innovative. The differentiator on the product side can be caught up, but to hire someone with thought leadership is not easy. Let's face it; there are more engineers than thought leaders in any start-up.

Once you understand what your superpower is, you can leverage your strength to capture the mindshare of customers. Building a community is a measurable process of gaining meaningful engagements with your customers and partners, and that is exactly what we did at Marketo. We built a community called Marketing Nation, a platform to help marketing practitioners and CMOs learn from their peers and share best practices with each other. We created content for the Marketing Nation community and attracted people to share stories within that community, from marketing manager to the marketing VP, through gamification. For example, a marketing VP shared her journey to be appointed to the CMO spot. She talked about how Marketo allowed her to track demand generation performance and turned data into actionable insights. Her story went viral within the community. She earned enough points to take one Marketo certification exam at no cost or receive a couple of Marketo swags. The more active people are, the more points they earn. We grew the community size by ten times within three years. It was fun, engaging, and rewarding.

This is a perfect example of how Marketo applied its strength to capture market share. It is where growth thrived at the intersection of technology and humanity.

Decision #18: How Will You Fill the Process Disconnect?

Hire your Sherpas, because you don't know what you don't know. When things don't go right, it is easy to make decisions based not on data, but on subjectivity. Having a data-driven decision-making process propels a company's growth. Cross-functional alignment with clear process mapping prevents people from playing the blame game.

What needs to be true for the organization to achieve your goals? What are the key metrics of success for each function?

Take a step back. What are one or two common metrics that get all the groups aligned so that each functional leader is in sync? You want everybody driving in the same direction. Consider this: If sales outperforms their numbers, we all get paid. If the customer is happy, we all get paid. If engineering is producing great products, we all get paid.

Filling the Process Disconnect sounds simple, like watching a dancer effortlessly leap across a stage. It looks easy, but it requires a tremendous amount of work, practice, and trust. **Establishing process and practice enables you to align strategy with execution while driving accountability.**

In the previous chapters, we discussed three disconnects: the Product/Market Fit Disconnect; Define Minimum Repeatability Disconnect; and Voice of Customer Disconnect. You have achieved initial success once you overcome these three disconnects. In a marathon, this is the part of the race you run with the pack. Most of the runners will still be in it at 13.2 miles. Overcoming the last two disconnects, however, will enable you to break away. Simply put, moving past the process and measurement disconnects will set you apart from others and lead you to ascend your start-up.

Now that you have reached the part of the journey where you have more customers and a bigger team, you have reached a milestone where you need to empower your team to internalize success through repeatable processes and dependable results.

Repeatability is your breakaway moment to scale. Repeatability is the engine that accelerates growth. You might wonder, at this point, why having a full sales funnel is not enough. Here's the reason: The key is not just lead generation, but moving those deals through the funnel like clockwork.

Conquering the Process Disconnect is the way through for go-to-market repeatability. You are looking at around 18 to 24 months for this part of the journey.

Be warned: This stage of the company is the hardest for first-time founders. It is where you are least experienced, meaning you have probably achieved certain milestones with the help of people you knew and trusted, maybe even from family and friends. However, at this stage, if you want to further align vision and strategy and scale, you have to rely on an experienced Sherpa who has scaled companies. You might not know them personally, or they might not even be people you would pick to have a Friday beer with. Taking it one step further, even though you follow and listen to them, the ride may not be a smooth one.

Decision #19: How Will You Fill the Measurement Disconnect?

Measure each function's performance so that "success" is rewarded consistently across your company. There's a science to it. It takes more than collecting enterprise logos to turn a start-up into a scale-up.

First comes key metrics under each area. Separate the leading indicator from lagging indicators. Earlier, we talked about the Ideal Customer Profile, whether you are B2B or

B2C, enterprise/midsize/small business, direct selling or multi-channel, brand positioning, and packaging. These are just a few indicators that bridge the Process Disconnect and enable you to align strategy with execution. During this part of your expedition, here are the questions you need to ask:

- What is our organizational strength?
- What are the desired business outcomes when applying our strength?
- What does this mean to each function?
- Are our strategic resources organized appropriately?
- Where might we find more strategic resources that will give us capabilities we do not have today?
- Does it work the same as our competitors?
- What is the backstory of our current situation?

Know your options. Here are the leading and lagging indicators.

Financials:

- Revenue, gross margin, operating expenses, and EBITDA for the quarter and YTD
- Income statement by functions (or P&L owners), with highlights on any significant trends, plus variances (positive or negative) between quarterly and YTD actuals and plan
- Covenant summary if your company has debt
- Balance sheet and cash flow summary
- Recurring revenue retention by month, quarter, and YTD, with highlights of lost and new customers and down sell.

- ○ Key cancellation and reduction—why the company is losing customers, where they are going, and strategies on how to prevent further losses
- ○ General and administration expenses for key initiatives

Sales:

- ○ Bookings performance by revenue type, deal type, and product in quarter/YTD compared to budget and previous year
- ○ Bookings performance by major geos
- ○ Sales rep and management productivity:
  - • Performance of each sales rep & regional sales leader over time (distinguish between new / tenured rep)
  - • Stack rank sales reps based on % quota achievement YTD
  - • Compare actual sales to forecast, quota, average, or some other benchmark—identify which reps are over/under plan
- ○ Pipeline: pipeline volume, quality, sales coverage, and conversation rate
- ○ Customer key wins and losses: Top customer wins and losses that occurred over the quarter. Understand why and how to repeat wins and prevent losses.
- ○ Sales rep territory maps: territory coverage, gaps, or strategies; how does it compare to competition?
- ○ Whitespace penetration: Track penetration of overall whitespace and market opportunities in the quarter and YTD

- Revenue contribution by partners
- Key competitive activities (competitor, size, strength, your winning strategy)
- The number of existing customers you have in multiple countries or products
- Average selling price and length of deal cycle
- Average time for sales rep onboarding and ramp
- Sales key initiatives impact vs. cost

Marketing:

- Revenue contribution: Marketing originated booking $ and %; Marketing influenced booking $ and %; Total bookings $ and % of overall bookings
- Spend: Overhead spend; Program spend; total marketing spend $ and %
- Lead generation: Marketing qualified leads (MQLs); % of MQLs accepted by sales; % of MQLs converted to deals
- Marketing programs impact vs. costs

Customer Success:

- Customer health by customer success manager, portfolio, and region
- Customer retention
- Product adoption
- Frequency and quality of customer interaction

Services:

- Service bookings, revenue, margin (current forecast vs. actual for quarter and YTD)
- Utilization rate by consulting resource type across Professional Services organization
- Average time taken to onboard customers by type by market by product
- Project delivery efficiency (onshore vs. offshore resources; managed services vs. consulting services)
- Service backlog by service revenue type by geo
- At-risk implementation % over total number of implementation trend; Reason for risks (i.e., Product, support, quality of services, etc.)
- Billable vs. Non-billable resource ratio
- Revenue per billable resource

Training:

- Type of training by function
- Certification program effectiveness
- Revenue by training program
- Customer, partner training effectiveness

Support:

- Booking, revenue, margin
- Number of cases by product and severity, average time for cases, productivity of support reps
- Breakdown of reasons for support cases
- NPS and CSAT
- Service Level Agreement percent completion

Product:

- Product development efficiency
- Development productivity and quality (Headcount by experience level, open customer defects, resource allocation)
- Product NPS

HR:

- Number of headcounts by department by month/quarter
- Attrition rate by department by month/quarter
- Performance ranking (top talents) by department
- Hiring funnel (number of candidates by department)

Other Important Measurements:

- Cybersecurity: Does your solution meet compliance requirements?
- Operation costs (i.e., cloud hosting, IT spend)
- Channel: Distribution, cost efficiency, productivity

Now, let's talk about a couple of measurements you can leverage to align strategy with execution and drive accountability:

- **COMPENSATION:** Is your compensation driving the right behavior? I worked for a company that had over 30% attrition rate consistently, yet the HR team was paid for 120% targeted bonus, while the customer success team was only paid less than 25% of target bonus and sales performance was decimal. Why? It was because the HR team was compensated based on the number of new hires. This means the higher the attrition rate, the more new hires will be recruited, and the higher the bonuses HR will receive. A financially savvy founder or an experienced CEO would have avoided this type of mistake.

- **NPS/CSAT/SLA:** What do you do with the NPS/CSAT/SLA score once you get it? Marketo is a great leader which holds the entire company accountable based on customer NPS and SLA. That contributed to its growth and longer-term success. I have worked with other companies, where there are multiple NPSs from the product team, support team, training/service team, and customer success team. No one shared what they learned from those surveys. It created an environment with a lack of accountability and resulted in high customer churn.

Decision #20: How Will You Measure the Company as a Customer-Centric Company?

First, how well do you know your customers? If your answer is, "We know our customers inside and out," then let me challenge you on that. (If you're feeling a little nervous, that's good; it means you care!) So, let's begin.

Do you have insights into each of your customers, their use cases, what they purchased and why, how much they spent on your solution, how well they adopted your solution, what the user persona is, a list of upsell and cross-sell opportunities;

the strength, weakness, threat, opportunity at your customer, and what that information means to you as a founder? (Wait, there's more.) Who does your account team interact with? Do you have relationships with executives and/or decision-makers? What is the NPS for your customer?

This may come as a surprise, but measuring customer-centricity does not just start with your customer; it starts internally with the employee experience. How well you treat your employees has a profound impact on their well-being and happiness. If they are satisfied with their job, feeling empowered and trusted, they will be dedicated to making customers happy. And doesn't "happy" sound like a great buzzword for a customer-centric company?

Decision #21: What Does Your Summit Look Like Now?

Investors might change. Key employees will move on. Your co-founder may leave you. You might pivot and find new ways to drive revenue. The Summit, in effect, moves. And that's OK and normal. No reason to throw down your pike and head back down the mountain. Life evolves. Your decisions leading to the Summit may change your course. So now, you must look again at your destination. How has it changed? What does it look like?

The biggest challenge for start-ups is the need to reprioritize what matters and accomplish operational must-dos with fewer resources and a limited budget. For example, the pandemic forced organizations to optimize the employee remote working experience in addition to reevaluating the customer experience. At the same time, organizations needed to be proactive on security operations because so much of what we do is being pushed through technology—virtual meetings, file-sharing, online collaboration tools, digital payments, and cloud technology. Priorities shifted for organizations to get their VPN connection and multi-factor authentication process in place, find tools that optimized employee communication and collaboration, and a host of events such as a disaster recovery plan, vendor succession planning, technology risk assessment, system backup, infrastructure and network stabilization, threat-identification and escalation procedures become priorities if they have not been in the past. You must update processes, procedures, and strategy accordingly for greater resilience, reliability, flexibility, and speed when driving the adoption of these new workplace protocols.

Lastly, you must know where you are going. It's frustrating not knowing what you're aiming for. Imagine flying blindfolded or getting in your car with no particular place to go. It's off-putting and scary. Tracking and measuring data will help you scale more fearlessly.

Onward

The decisions in this chapter lead you to the Summit. They will help you to establish processes and practices that align strategy with execution and scale up your success with measurements to drive accountability. The truth is, the strategy may have shifted since you first began. Have the courage and acumen to go back down the mountain and reevaluate, because as you leave the Align Strategy with Process and Measurement Camp, you want to get clearer about translating vision into strategy—what to take with you, what not to do, and who will be by your side. This is how you build processes that stick and turn strategy into execution (a.k.a. action!).

My execution plan had to change when I crossed the river. I was forced to ask tough questions: What does it mean to cross that river? If I turn back, what does that feel like?

I didn't know how far away from the flagpole I was. I was willing to try another mile, another hour before I turned back. I went through the process of risk assessment and potential payoff for my decision. If I failed, what would I be doing? If I succeeded, how would I feel?

In the end, I was incredibly proud I carried those ashes forward. I didn't pack everything right. A cashmere sweater, the most inexpensive one I could find, made sweat cling to my skin like thorns. Once I crossed the river, I had to take my freezing, soaking wet jeans off. Bad choice of clothes. But I *could* pull my snowsuit from my backpack. Amid packing errors, the fact remained that I was prepared. Many people didn't cross the river because they were not prepared. They had no choice but to give up.

To be in a position with no options is the worst position of all. If there's one thing I can leave with you right now about scaling the start-up mountain, it's this: Throughout your ascent, my friend, you have choices. Take them. Face the onslaught of decisions with thoughtfulness and confidence. One wrong decision could give your competitor an edge, weaken a key customer relationship, or even put you out of business. Check your ego at the door. Then, keep going.

Chapter 7

THE SUMMIT: A VIEW TOWARD YOUR NEXT PEAK

After the climb, I feel a sense of double grief. One is the loss of my grandmother. The other is the finality of my last gesture for her. I've done everything she has asked of me. I think to myself: *What will I do next?*

I begin to feel a little lost. I wish Grandma were here to fill the empty space inside. I wonder: How will I stay special?

When I think of the founder's journey, I believe that growth thrives at the intersection of technology and humanity. You need to define what "staying special" means for you, and how you remain close to your "why." This will set you miles apart from the pack.

The Summit

Your climb will ultimately put you on the global stage. I want you to imagine that. Technology must be driven by vision and wisdom and implemented by the right people. To be on the global stage, you must take your team with you—every person from every part of your organization. You must strive for tremendous clarity, efficiency of core practices, and show why you are making that journey so that it matters to everyone on your team in the same way it matters to you. You must create believers, because everything will not go as planned. Believers will stay with you even when they can't see what is in front of them ... and even when things go wrong.

All of this leads to one thing: scaling your start-up faster and more fearlessly so you reach the Summit—however you define it.

Decision #22: How Will You Inspire Cultural Collaboration?

Cultural Collaboration means taking intentional action to build an inclusive, thriving culture where it's safe to share ideas. Both words are capitalized—with Cultural coming first—on purpose. Collaborative culture is described as a culture where "collaboration is intentional and deliberate," according to Atlassian.[1] Evan Rosen, author of *The Culture of Collaboration: Maximizing Time, Talent and Tools to Create*

---

[1]"How to Create a Collaborative Culture," Atlassian, https://www.atlassian .com/work-management/project-management/project-execution/collaborative -culture

Value in the Global Economy, points out that trust is key to making a collaborative culture work. There's no question about it.[1]

None of that, however, is enough.

I've taken a different approach. I've reversed the two words. While collaborative culture sounds good, Cultural Collaboration begins with a thoughtful commitment to culture first and foremost as a way to bring people together. Start with a minimal viable culture where you don't try to boil the ocean all in one day but rather set down a simple set of shared beliefs for stakeholders to lean on in order to create remarkable outcomes.

Company culture drives sustainable growth. Central to that is the employee experience, which leads to a better customer experience. This matters not just some of the time, but *all* of the time. Aligning strategy to day-to-day execution is critical. This means clarifying roles and responsibilities, setting up expectations, holding people accountable, rewarding top performers, and weeding out toxic employees.

Creating a culture of learning to encourage employees to help one another, cultivate gratitude, practice transparency, and understand how each employee can contribute to the overall company success inspires real disruption that leads to a new way of thinking and defines your start-up inside and out. No matter how technologically advanced your company,

[1] Evan Rosen, "The Culture of Collaboration," IndustryWeek, Published January 11, 2007, https://www.industryweek.com/leadership/companies-executives /article/21940813/the-culture-of-collaboration

only 20 percent of your success is attributed to your technology, and 80 percent is overcoming the change management necessary to operationalize your vision. Why? Because growth thrives at the intersection of humanity and technology. That's why Cultural Collaboration is so imperative. Here are a few things you need to take into consideration when it comes to Cultural Collaboration.

Inclusion and Cultural Collaboration

It's important to be an ally for people who are underrepresented. Stand up for them. Being quiet, even when you disagree with others, does not encourage positive change.

With the disparagingly low numbers of women and minorities in the field of technology, allies have the opportunity to lift others up. The burden is not, however, solely on them. I've mentored and coached many women tech leaders. We have a tendency to give of our time freely and graciously. Men are better at creating boundaries. I find they say "no" more freely. It's a good habit to have because you need the mindset, the thinking time to dream.

Women emerge as stronger leaders when they support each other and promote each other. A water drop in the ocean won't create any ripples, but a wave is a force of nature. I love communities like the Athena Alliance, Him for Her, and Women In Technology. They are rallying women in tech and saying, "Look, we have to change the culture. We have to hire more women in tech careers, find more investment dollars for female tech founders, and advance more women to the boardrooms."

Over my career, I've seen many women who don't support other women. That's a problem. When we support each other, we become a stronger force. The journey is hard enough. Without the support of other women, it makes it hard for all.

Ask yourself:

- Do people in your start-up feel valued?
- Do those who are underrepresented have a voice?
- How are you championing people who are under-represented?

Investors and Cultural Collaboration

Look at potential investors and their track record. You get to decide who you work with. Understand your investor's culture and decision criteria. What is the success rate in their portfolio? Are they bottom-line driven or top-line driven? Is there pressure on the financials or longer-term success? Are they global or US only? Do they have operating principles to guide you toward growth? Who are the people in their network, and what is their reputation? Investors take different approaches. The experienced investment firm, however, calls people within your company; they don't just listen to your pitch. They evaluate and determine if the fit has endurance and aligns with their core criteria.

Ask yourself:

- What is the track record of a potential investor?
- How much control would you like to give to your investor?
- What values do you have in common?

- Does the investor have the complimentary capability you need beyond funding?
- When you find an investor that is not a good fit, how do you define the relationship going forward?

Hiring and Cultural Collaboration

Hiring the right people to fit the culture will set you apart. Have you ever worked in a place where you felt like making a suggestion was risky business? Innovation is thwarted when there's a stifled culture. Partner with new hires so they succeed as well as your company.

Oftentimes, there's tremendous pressure from the board or investors to hire, but you must slow down. A more thoughtful hire is better. Tech-savvy founders need people with business experience to complement the start-up build. Partner for the long run, not the short term.

I have a friend who worked for a start-up where the founder cycled through executives right before they approached their vesting schedule. Their founders owned limited shares of equity and had to let go of executives, reallocating equities to the next hire. That's an ethical problem. The company experienced high customer churns for a while before it went out of business. You should always treat others the way you want to be treated. Set up the right expectations. As you prepare to scale, let people know you are all on the same team. Communicate what your brand stands for. Lay out the expectations and concerns—before you get so far away from where you came from and before you start this next leg of the journey.

On a high-altitude mountain, the person who is most fit may not make it. You can't judge people on what they say they've done in the past, how they look, or what their resume says. Instead, work with a person for three months before you hire them. That gives you time to figure out if the fit feels right. I have a strong personality, for instance. I say what I think, which stems from a deep sense of commitment. For some founders, that's a bad fit. If that's the case, then hiring someone more green to take orders might be a good idea.

Ask yourself:

- How do your hiring practices encourage cultural collaboration?
- If you were describing your company to a new hire, how would you describe your culture?
- How often do you do employee surveys?
- What action have you taken to improve based on the employee surveys?

Leadership and Cultural Collaboration

Some founders find it difficult to express their own opinions, or they only say what people want to hear. That's dangerous because, again, you cannot encourage positive change without honesty. To scale faster and more fearlessly, real conversations take the place of superficial exchanges. You betray the trust of all when you break the trust of one person. People are watching. Your leadership team is watching. A lack of trust impedes your start-up's journey and holds you back.

I've seen leaders who encourage Cultural Collaboration, and I've seen leaders who are the polar opposite. For lack of a better word, the latter category might be called bullies, and bullies never win in the end. Their sales tank. Their retention stinks. Their websites dissolve, and no one cares. You are the leader who sets the tone for the culture. Encourage suggestions. This is what innovation is all about! You want opinions. Curiosity is your competitive advantage, and diverse opinions lead to greater innovation.

Isn't being an innovator part of why you started this climb in the first place?

Resilient leadership also means letting go sometimes. Are you willing to let others lead the expedition? Will you believe in people, even if they've never mastered a particular milestone before?

When Oracle was in acquisition mode (there were 83 companies acquired in the 4 years I was there), I was tapped to serve in different roles. There were some I was fluent in, and some were completely new. I simply had never done them before. However, they believed I could learn fast, and they were right. Had I stuck with what I knew, or if I didn't have leaders who believed in me, I would never have been a solution architect on the North America Strategic Account ("NASA") sales team (which was absolutely a phenomenal experience).

It's hard to let go when you are a founder. We've all seen insecurity and ego stand in the way of company growth. Will you succumb to these distracting voices, or will you let go and trust your team, your idea, and the journey?

When you put your life into other people's hands, you have to trust. In a mountain environment, you are between life and death. You either listen to and work with others, or you die.

When you've invested every penny of your money, your life's work, and your time, leading may seem synonymous with doing it all yourself, but this is a hard way to go.

Ask yourself:

- Are you willing to trust others to enable growth?
- How do you inspire Cultural Collaboration as a leader?
- In what ways does your culture encourage innovation?
- Do you have truthful and transparent conversations with others?
- Do you speak up, even when it's uncomfortable?

Gratitude and Cultural Collaboration

Focusing on positivity means cultivating gratitude. When you're grateful, you're focused on building relationships.

For the past decade, I've started my day by writing three thank-you notes. I start with positivity and an expression of my values. Being one who is a strong advocate for measuring performance, I would also have to say that much of what I have today came from being grateful. I don't often give gifts, but I *do* send notes. These notes carry weight with people. It has made a profound impact on my direct reports or others on my team. Early on, I had great managers. Many wrote simple notes of appreciation to me, which I have kept.

Ask yourself:

- What role does gratitude play in your culture?
- How do you show gratitude to others?
- What kind of gratitude practice do you follow to reward top performers?

Empathy and Cultural Collaboration

When I was a consultant at Hyperion, I used to be like a Navy SEAL from a technical perspective. They sent me to a customer site—a bank in Columbus, Ohio—where the newly released system had crashed after running for 19 hours. Our customer was *not* happy. They were going to throw the software away and end the relationship.

When I walked into the conference room, I noticed it was all angry men … and me. They were surprised when they saw me walk in, a petite Asian woman, and even more surprised at what I said: "This feels like a funeral. Am I in the right place?" I took a gamble, but I knew I had to get their attention. My opening line did the trick.

Then I continued. "I know how you feel. Let's get to work." I handed out a Post-It note to each of them and posed the question: "Why did you invest in Hyperion in the first place?" I collected the notes and read them out loud. Positivity started to enter the room like little slants of sunshine, and empathy unified us.

After our positivity exercise, I gave them another task. "Crashing after 19 hours is not acceptable. But you have to work with me on this. Here's what we'll do. I'll split the team into two. Team one manages design review. Team two focuses on data backup."

Fifteen hours later, the system was redesigned and calculated correctly within thirty seconds. I saved the beautiful notes they sent afterward. They remind me to see things through and to invite others to walk alongside me, even in really hard times.

Fact: Things go wrong in life. However, the way you handle a tough situation has a lasting impact on everyone. First, acknowledge the challenge others face. Then get a plan and rally the support to fix it.

By the time I walked into that conference room to consult the bank, I had designed more than 400 systems, so, experience, of course, counts. Obviously, I knew going in that there was hope, and I did a lot of homework beforehand. Empathy, however, was just as important. You can't help people who don't listen. They blamed everything on the product, which is completely understandable. However, the technology was designed and built by our partner, who didn't have a deep knowledge of the newly released version of our product.

Not only did I fix the problem, but I reached out to the partner before *and* after. It made them better and stronger, and our partner benefited as well.

Ask yourself:

- What is one story where empathy played an important role in your culture?
- What does empathy mean to you?
- How do you inspire empathy in others?

Decision #23: How Has Your Technology Connected Humanity in a Better or Bigger Way?

Technology needs to have a more meaningful way to help people.

The onset of the pandemic was an epic test of character and leadership. During the first few months, many leaders I spoke to felt powerless and unprepared. Now, most are seizing the moment to adapt, stay ahead, and emerge stronger. The pandemic has forced our hand to better understand our purpose. KPMG/Forbes Insights survey stated that, since the pandemic, 79% of CEOs have had to re-evaluate their brand's purpose to better address the needs of stakeholders.

We have now entered the Era of the Customer Relationship. We've gotten back to what is important to people. One of my core philosophies is that growth thrives at the intersection of tech and humanity.

As exciting as technology is, it is good to remember Maslow's Hierarchy of Needs: physiological, safety, love and belonging, esteem, and self-actualization. Our well-being and safety are the most important. At the intersection of tech and humanity, technology needs to support the goals of *real* people. If you're not sure how your brand and technology aids humanity, it's time to more deeply explore your beliefs around the industry you are helping to drive: Does technology help or hinder humanity?

Inspiring others to live their purpose through your technology is one of the most important gestures of love you can give people. I can't underscore this enough. When people are unhappy, it is oftentimes because they are unfulfilled. And I believe, when this happens, it's because we are not in alignment with our purpose. So, how does your technology fill that gap?

Here's something to think about.

Technology is a path to freedom. It frees people to explore and live their purpose. Let me give you a hypothetical example. Let's say Jessica, who is a hard worker and has been on the marketing demand gen team for over three years, realizes that her "why" is to connect execution with go-to-market strategy and drive company growth. Every time she is engaged in growth strategy discussions, it lights her up! Time stops when she does this. But time drags on when she has to answer administrative questions or do other mundane tasks that weigh down her day. If technology helps her bypass those tasks and creates more time in her schedule to live her purpose and have more strategic growth strategy conversations, she can make a bigger impact and have more uninterrupted time to sketch out what the future looks like for her sales partner and the company's bottom line.

Can you imagine how successful she will be? I can. I see this every day with technology. I see it with myself. When I use technology that emboldens me, allows me to live my purpose and not become burdened with the things that don't align with my "why," then I am free to multiply success for the people I work with.

In BCG's article describing the "age of the bionic company," the authors make a profound point by saying:[1]

> *For all that machines will change us, humans will remain the essence of companies. In fact, the real power of a bionic company lies in further unleashing the power of human creativity. Machines are only enablers.*

[1]Rich Hutchinson, Lionel Aré, Justin Rose, and Allison Bailey, "The Bionic Company," Published November 7, 2019, https://www.bcg.com/publications/2019/bionic-company

What about you? Why are *you* on this journey as a start-up founder? How is your technology making a difference for humanity?

Decision #24: How Will You Armor Up for Adversity?

In the face of adversity, we are who we choose to be.

One of the greatest setbacks that founders encounter is the word "no." Investors hit delete on your deck. Customers abandon carts. Team members leave. Supply chain partners go dark. Nobody likes to be told "no." But I'd like to challenge you that when hearing the word "no," you should also hear the word "yes." The ability to figure out what to listen to and take to heart sets successful founders apart from others.

No matter where you are in your journey, you must recognize that there will be lots of personal sacrifice, and you will often want to give up. The obstacles number like the stars: government, taxation, competition, employees who may try to steal ideas or customers, products that don't work, missed delivery dates, customer backlash, the board of advisors that demands more and investors pounding on you to generate X amount.

There are days you put forth a lot of effort, and there is no reward. Sometimes, you simply don't know if you can or cannot produce, but you have to show confidence with your investors and your leadership team. One off moment can push you off the mountain. You need to stay focused on what's within your control. Focus on what matters. Focus on your why.

While climbing an ice glacier, the crampon, a small piece of metal in the sole of my shoe, broke. You'll know when that moment hits, when you make one mistake that could have massive consequences. (My rope saved me as I dangled off the face of that glacier!) In business, maybe you are off in the market, and demand is not there. Like my ice climbing expedition, you hire someone who has been there and done that. On this journey, there's no Rx or magic. You must leverage the experts' frameworks and apply them to your business. They can point out how to turn those off moments into pivotal moments.

Here are four actions you can take to armor up for adversity:

1. **Look Up.** It takes determination to overcome the challenges you will face as a founder. We all know there is no straight line to the summit—but you have to believe, and you have to inspire others to believe with you.

   Share the big vision and show others what the peak looks like. You might fail—and that's OK. Don't be afraid to admit defeat the first time around.
   Prepare your physical self and your mindset. When I saw the map, it was intimidating on Everest. Breaking it down into shorter stints in my mind made it achievable.

2. **Prepare and Stay the Course.** Do you have the grit to see this expedition through? Grit is defined as unyielding courage in the face of hardship. But who teaches us grit? Where do we find it? How do we develop it?

   In the Asian culture, we are taught the values of courtesy, piety, and benevolence. These enduring qualities are good and sacred, but they must also live in harmony with our ability to overcome challenges with courage. This is where our grit lives and breathes. This is where we find unbounded success, life fulfillment, and our best selves. On days when everything is going well, grit may never show her hand. In the face of our most challenging moments, however, grit almost always asks to be heard.

When we doubt our abilities, encounter impossible challenges, or face circumstances beyond our control, we naturally hold a mirror to our inner courage. What do we see? The person who has been shaped by your experiences and the choice you made to live with grit. The truth is, grit has been inside you all along. It's just a matter of finding it. Preparing the way with resilience transforms a mediocre performer into a top performer. Preparing for our climb meant wearing the right clothes, packing the right things, communicating with each other, trusting one another, fueling ourselves with the right energy, and learning about the road ahead.

3. **Celebrate Small Wins.** Scaling your start-up is precarious and hard, both mentally and physically. It is easy to get frustrated when you don't see a result, so you need to encourage your team and celebrate small achievements. While there's cause for celebration when you reach the peak, there should be celebrations along the way at each milestone: new customer wins, kudos from customers, team accomplishments, individual growth, hitting KPIs, etc.

4. **Inspire Believers and Work Together.** What is the role of ego in your climb? Many founders, while they can turn an idea into a product, fail when it comes to listening and challenging. Instead, they listen in an echo chamber.

Engineers, which many tech founders are, don't always ask the right growth-related questions, challenging aligning strategy to execution.

I know one founder who is very arrogant. She has published many papers and is a university professor. She did not respect anyone. Many of the people she hired left. Sometimes pride gets in the way. In another case, a founder would talk for two and a half hours during a three-hour meeting. He could not take a difference of opinion without screaming, so no one spoke up. He would only get an echo chamber. Conversely, the founders of Marketo and Jebbit listen to others, respect and inspire their teams. That resulted in growth acceleration.

Decision #25: How Will You Handle the Loneliness Factor?

People generally have a hard time understanding the demands of being a founder. Find an advisor, a thought partner, or someone to seek best practices with. Build a community.

Self-assurance is not ego; rather, it is a quiet confidence that fills the void of being at the top, which is, by virtue of the position, a solo act. Scaling the tech start-up mountain is both a solitary and rewarding journey for C-suite executives. Not everyone you started the journey with makes it with you. This might even include family or friends. Colleagues who are not founders may not understand the pressures and challenges you face. This is another reason why making time for your family (and making time for yourself) is critical.

The pile of unfinished work will never go away. The demands on you will not evaporate. There will always be one more thing to do or one more person to call. Having your go-to people builds a moat around the loneliness you might feel and creates a more joyful life journey as well. Reading, hobbies, exercise, volunteering in your community, mentoring others at local innovation centers are all ways to take an edge off the loneliness founders sometimes feel.

Decision #26: How Will You Take Care of and Preserve Yourself?

You must clearly understand the mission ahead. Climbers must scale the mountain while keeping themselves alive. So, too, must founders. Sometimes, though, it's easy to forget how important it is to keep both your employees and you sane while scaling a start-up. This can cause burnout, unwanted company culture, missteps, and even illness.

Ascending a mountain is not where you lose lives. It's coming down. While people have the energy to go up, it's easy to forget that you have to come back down. It's like a marathon—not a sprint.

You are probably sprinting right now. Working 80 hours a week, taking calls on the weekends, getting up early in the hopes you can catch up, but, funny thing, it never works. There's always more of everything. The piles around your desk are tamed, never banished.

Overworking is an outgrowth of going from idea to product. There are so many things to get done, and you are a skeleton crew of so few.

I did this, too. And now I know it was a mistake.

We are passionate about what we do. However, when you love your work more than yourself, you put the company and your employees in danger. You have to reserve some energy. Yes, give "100%," but you need to save 10% for the people you love (including you) for the climb down. The psychological impact of coming down makes you feel even more exhausted. It requires a lot of finesse. You have to take care of yourself, even when it's easier not to. Mountain climber Alison Levine hates butter, but ate it as fat to burn so she could reserve energy.

I learned the potential dangers of overdoing it on a hot summer day in June. I was running a virtual customer round table via Zoom call, and had been working long hours leading up to that day. As I was coming out of the restroom, I hit my head so hard, I was out. I slept for 19 hours. Still, I went on like nothing had happened and went back to work. I went on a 10-mile bike ride that same weekend. The following week, my head pain got worse, so I called the nurse. The doctor was afraid of internal bleeding, so they put me through a CT scan.

Was it all worth it? That's not the question. Did pouring all my energy and time into my work mean I accomplished more?

Absolutely not.

Anything extra I did caused me to go backward, and not in a good way. When you work so much and get yourself injured out of exhaustion, it's a reflection of what you should not be doing in the first place. The output won't be where you want it to be. When you run the business, you don't have extra energy.

It's important to take a break and preserve your energy. Stepping back, reflecting, and setting up the right example for others matters. Being exhausted will not help you solve the problem or live your purpose. Being overworked leads to burnout, and burnout keeps you from reaching the Summit.

Take some time and make space for yourself, then extend this culture to your team. Ask: How do I build an environment where the talent can help us do more than we can achieve alone?

I hope you never hit your head like I did, but when you feel exhausted, it is the sign you need to take a break.

Onward

You don't have to wait until you get to the peak to celebrate. In fact, you shouldn't. Find measurable milestones and celebrate along the way. Why? Because celebrating gives you something to look forward to, and it makes the ascent up the start-up mountain a lot more enjoyable!

A LOOK BACK
AT THE MOUNTAIN

Scaling your start-up is not about title, status, or even money; rather, it is the ability to inspire and motivate others to achieve a common goal. It is pursuing your "why," as we learned in chapter one, and inspiring customers and employees to live their purpose at the crossroad of tech and humanity. While the Valley of Disconnects is littered with unknowns, you now know what many of them are, and that knowledge alone arms you with the foresight to slay them one by one.

In the Turn Idea into Product Camp, we learned it isn't a sprint, but rather a marathon, starting with your MVP and the Define-Minimum Repeatability Disconnect. One of the most critical steps here is defining your problem statement while also focusing on what kind of company you want to build and mapping out your culture, value, and brand.

The Move Product to Market Camp moved us forward and challenged you to explore your minimal viable team, a pivotal moment when learning from others becomes imperative. Find your Sherpa. From there, build an engine to drive repeatable sales so you reach the next milestone, the Go From Market to Scale Camp. Repeatability is what takes you from market to scale as you conquer the Product/Market Fit Disconnect.

Perhaps the most important camp of all was found in chapter five. It is, I have to confess, the one I feel makes or breaks long-term success for virtually any company. This is, of course, the Acclimate to The Voice of Customer Camp. If you know the people you serve (and this includes your employees as well as your customers), your climb is exponentially more vibrant, fun and results-driven. The Customer Voice Disconnect defines the founder who is hungry to take the honorable path to the Summit.

In the Align Strategy With Process and Measurement Camp, you took all that you had learned and applied measurements to many of those points. Keeping people accountable across the organization puts you in the top performer class and helps you slay both the Process Disconnect and Measurement Disconnect.

Lastly, we looked at the mental and physical rigors of being a founder and asked the tough questions to keep you sane and ready to view, not just the summit you will reach, but the peaks beyond.

FINAL THOUGHTS

Growing up in China, where males are revered, gave me the grit to stay the course. I was the youngest of nine children in the house and the only girl. If I wanted to be heard, I had no choice but to be resilient to failure and persistent in my "ask."

You, as a founder, also have this grit inside you, or you wouldn't be reading this book right now. Successful founders listen to experienced people, care about their employees, embrace failure as learning moments, and do not consider "no" a nasty word (they hear the "yes" in that little word!). They know there's always another peak to scale because that's the wondrous thing about any mountain. There is always another one to dominate. Same goes for our companies. Same goes for us in life.

What three words does your brand stand for? This is your legacy. For me, I want to be a multiplier. If this were my last day on earth, I would hope the people left behind say that I made their lives better in measurable ways and that I multiplied their joy, prosperity, and knowledge.

This is my promise to you: Summiting the mountain is not the end of your journey. Coming down safely with your entire team and celebrating the accomplishment is where you want to be in the end. This means having meaningful interactions with people you work with, having fun, enjoying the journey, and never forgetting the people who are generating and benefiting from an excellent customer experience.

To all the founders, stay special. Make the world proud. Define what staying special means to *you*. It took me years to understand this. At the intersection of tech and humanity, that's where growth thrives. That's where you will shine. That's where you will take technology to new heights and leave an unforgettable footprint as you scale faster and more fearlessly.

ABOUT HELEN YU

An advisor to the world's largest technology companies, Helen Yu passionately believes growth comes at the crossroad of tech and humanity. Whether she is speaking to a crowd of 5,000 or a small start-up leadership, she brings global customer success experience from her work with tech titans like Oracle, Adobe, and many start-up CEOs who went on to achieve multibillion-dollar revenue growth and record profitability.

As the Founder and CEO at Tigon Advisory, Helen drives growth for the largest technology companies in the world and is a board advisor to fast growth SaaS companies. She serves as Vice Chair and Board Director at the Global Cybersecurity Association.

A highly respected thought leader, she is a top Twitter influencer in AI, Cloud, IoT, Cybersecurity, 5G, Growth, FinTech and Start-ups with a weekly reach of more than 10M. Helen is recognized as a global thought leader by organizations including IBM and Thinkers360. She speaks regularly at conferences including SXSW, TiECon, Global AI and Big Data conference, DMS, and Money2020.